# KIDS' FAVORITE
## Classroom Treats

## Publications International, Ltd.

Favorite Brand Name Recipes at www.fbnr.com

**Pictured on the front cover:** Ice Cream Cone Cupcakes *(page 160)*.
**Pictured on the back cover** *(clockwise from top):* Quick S'More *(page 156)*, Peanut Butter Bear *(page 6)* and Domino Cookies *(page 40)*.

**Microwave Cooking:** Microwave ovens vary in wattage. Use the cooking times as guidelines and check for doneness before adding more time.

**Preparation/Cooking Times:** Preparation times are based on the approximate amount of time required to assemble the recipe before cooking, baking, chilling or serving. These times include preparation steps such as measuring, chopping and mixing. The fact that some preparations and cooking can be done simultaneously is taken into account. Preparation of optional ingredients and serving suggestions is not included.

# CONTENTS

# Bake Sale Bounty

## Crayon Cookies

   1 cup butter, softened
   2 teaspoons vanilla
   ½ cup powdered sugar
2¼ cups all-purpose flour
   ¼ teaspoon salt
     Assorted paste food colorings
1½ cups chocolate chips
1½ teaspoons shortening

**1.** Preheat oven to 350°F. Grease cookie sheets.

**2.** Beat butter and vanilla in large bowl at high speed of electric mixer until fluffy. Add powdered sugar; beat at medium speed until blended. Combine flour and salt in small bowl. Gradually add to butter mixture.

**3.** Divide dough into 10 equal sections. Reserve 1 section; cover and refrigerate remaining 9 sections. Combine reserved section and desired food coloring in small bowl; blend well.

**4.** Cut dough in half. Roll each half into 5-inch log. Pinch one end to resemble crayon tip. Place cookies 2 inches apart on prepared cookie sheets. Repeat with remaining 9 sections of dough and desired food colorings.

**5.** Bake 15 to 18 minutes or until edges are lightly browned. Cool completely on cookie sheets.

**6.** Combine chocolate chips and shortening in small microwavable bowl. Microwave at HIGH 1 to 1½ minutes, stirring after 1 minute, or until smooth. Decorate cookies with chocolate mixture to look like crayons. *Makes 20 cookies*

# Peanut Butter Bears

2 cups uncooked quick oats

2 cups all-purpose flour

1 tablespoon baking powder

1 cup granulated sugar

¾ cup butter, softened

½ cup creamy peanut butter

½ cup packed brown sugar

½ cup cholesterol-free egg substitute

1 teaspoon vanilla

3 tablespoons miniature chocolate chips

**1.** Stir together rolled oats, flour and baking powder; set aside.

**2.** Beat granulated sugar, butter, peanut butter and brown sugar in large mixer bowl with mixer at medium-high speed until creamed. Add egg substitute and vanilla; beat until light and fluffy. Add rolled oat mixture. Beat on low speed until combined. Cover and refrigerate 1 to 2 hours or until easy to handle.

**3.** Preheat oven to 375°F.

**4.** For each bear, shape one 1-inch ball for body and one ¾-inch ball for head. Place body and head together on baking sheet; flatten slightly. Make 7 small balls for ears, arms, legs and mouth. Place on bear body and head. Place 2 chocolate chips on each head for eyes; place 1 chocolate chip on each body for belly-button.

**5.** Bake 9 to 11 minutes or until light brown. Cool 1 minute on cookie sheet. Remove to wire racks; cool completely.

*Makes 4 dozen cookies*

**Peanut Butter Bear**

# Bamboozlers

1 cup all-purpose flour

¾ cup packed light brown sugar

¼ cup unsweetened cocoa powder

1 egg

2 egg whites

5 tablespoons margarine, melted

¼ cup fat-free (skim) milk

¼ cup honey

1 teaspoon vanilla

2 tablespoons semisweet chocolate chips

2 tablespoons coarsely chopped walnuts

Powdered sugar (optional)

**1.** Preheat oven to 350°F. Grease and flour 8-inch square baking pan; set aside.

**2.** Combine flour, brown sugar and cocoa in medium bowl. Blend together egg, egg whites, margarine, milk, honey and vanilla in medium bowl. Add to flour mixture; mix well. Pour into prepared baking pan; sprinkle with chocolate chips and walnuts.

**3.** Bake brownies until they spring back when lightly touched in center, about 30 minutes. Cool completely in pan on wire rack. Sprinkle with powdered sugar just before serving.

*Makes 1 dozen brownies*

**Peanutters:** Substitute peanut butter chips for chocolate chips and peanuts for walnuts.

**Butterscotch Babies:** Substitute butterscotch chips for chocolate chips and pecans for walnuts.

**Brownie Sundaes:** Serve brownies on dessert plates. Top each brownie with a scoop of vanilla nonfat frozen yogurt and 2 tablespoons nonfat chocolate or caramel sauce.

# Worm Cookies

**1¾ cups all-purpose flour**

**¾ cup powdered sugar**

**¼ cup unsweetened cocoa powder**

**⅛ teaspoon salt**

**1 cup butter**

**1 teaspoon vanilla**

**1 tube white frosting**

**1.** Combine flour, sugar, cocoa and salt; set aside. Combine butter and vanilla in large bowl. Beat with electric mixer at medium-low speed until fluffy. Gradually beat in flour mixture until well combined. Cover and chill dough at least 30 minutes before rolling.

**2.** Preheat oven to 350°F. Form dough into 1½ inch balls. Roll balls gently to form 5- to 6-inch logs about ½ inch thick. Shape into worms 2 inches apart on ungreased cookie sheets.

**3.** Bake 12 minutes or until set. Let stand on cookie sheets until cooled completely. Make eyes and stripes with white frosting.

*Makes about 3 dozen cookies*

# Pots of Gold

1 package (18 ounces) refrigerated sugar cookie dough
¼ cup unsweetened cocoa powder
Prepared white frosting
Green and black food coloring
Yellow miniature candy-coated chocolate pieces

**1.** Preheat oven to 350°F. Remove dough from wrapper; place in large bowl. Add cocoa powder; beat until well blended.

**2.** Roll dough on lightly floured surface to ⅛-inch thickness. Cut out pots with 4-inch cookie cutter. (Halloween cauldron cookie cutter may be used.)

**3.** Place cookies 2 inches apart on ungreased baking sheets. Bake about 6 minutes or until firm. Cool on baking sheets 2 minutes. Remove to wire racks; cool completely.

**4.** Spoon ⅔ of frosting into small bowl; tint with green food coloring. Spoon remaning ⅓ of frosting into small bowl; tint with black food coloring. Frost bottom of pot in green; top of pot in black. Arrange yellow candies over black frosting to resemble gold.

*Makes about 2½ dozen cookies*

# Ice Skates

½ cup (1 stick) butter, softened

1¼ cups honey

1 cup packed brown sugar

1 egg, separated

5½ cups self-rising flour

1 teaspoon ground ginger

1 teaspoon ground cinnamon

½ cup milk

Assorted colored icings, candies and small candy canes

**1.** Beat butter, honey, brown sugar and egg yolk in large bowl at medium speed of electric mixer until light and fluffy.

**2.** Combine flour, ginger and cinnamon in small bowl. Add alternately with milk to butter mixture; beat just until combined. Cover; refrigerate 30 minutes.

**3.** Preheat oven to 350°F. Grease cookie sheets.

**4.** Roll dough on lightly floured surface to ¼-inch thickness. Cut out dough using 3½-inch boot-shaped cookie cutter. Place cutouts 2 inches apart on prepared cookie sheets.

**5.** Bake 8 to 10 minutes or until lightly browned. Cool 2 minutes on cookie sheets. Remove to wire racks; cool completely.

**6.** Decorate cookies with colored icings and candies to look like ice skates, attaching candy canes as skate blades.

*Makes about 4 dozen cookies*

# Chocolate Crackletops

2 cups all-purpose flour

2 teaspoons baking powder

2 cups granulated sugar

½ cup (1 stick) butter or margarine

4 squares (1 ounce each) unsweetened baking chocolate, chopped

4 large eggs, lightly beaten

2 teaspoons vanilla extract

1¾ cups "M&M's"® Chocolate Mini Baking Bits

Additional granulated sugar

Combine flour and baking powder; set aside. In 2-quart saucepan over medium heat combine 2 cups sugar, butter and chocolate, stirring until butter and chocolate are melted; remove from heat. Gradually stir in eggs and vanilla. Stir in flour mixture until well blended. Chill mixture 1 hour. Stir in "M&M's"® Chocolate Mini Baking Bits; chill mixture an additional 1 hour.

Preheat oven to 350°F. Line cookie sheets with foil. With sugar-dusted hands, roll dough into 1-inch balls; roll balls in additional granulated sugar. Place about 2 inches apart onto prepared cookie sheets. Bake 10 to 12 minutes. Do not overbake. Cool completely on wire racks. Store in tightly covered container.

*Makes about 5 dozen cookies*

# nutty Footballs

- **1 cup butter, softened**
- **½ cup sugar**
- **1 egg**
- **½ teaspoon vanilla**
- **2 cups all-purpose flour**
- **¼ cup unsweetened cocoa powder**
- **1 cup finely chopped almonds**
- **Colored icings (optional)**
- **White icing**

**1.** Beat butter and sugar in large bowl until creamy. Add egg and vanilla; mix until well blended. Stir together flour and cocoa; gradually add to butter mixture, beating until well blended. Add almonds; beat until well blended. Shape dough into disc. Wrap dough in plastic wrap and refrigerate 30 minutes.

**2.** Preheat oven to 350°F. Lightly grease cookie sheets. Roll out dough on floured surface to ¼-inch thickness. Cut dough with 2½- to 3-inch football-shaped cookie cutter.* Place 2 inches apart on prepared cookie sheets.

**3.** Bake 10 to 12 minutes or until set. Cool on cookie sheets 1 to 2 minutes. Remove to wire racks; cool completely. Decorate with colored icings, if desired. Pipe white icing onto footballs to make laces.

*Makes 2 dozen cookies*

*If you do not have a football-shaped cookie cutter, shape 3 tablespoonfuls of dough into ovals. Place 3 inches apart on prepared cookie sheets. Flatten ovals to ¼-inch thickness; taper ends. Bake as directed.*

# Peanut Butter and Chocolate Spirals

    1 package (20 ounces) refrigerated sugar cookie dough
    1 package (20 ounces) refrigerated peanut butter cookie dough
    ¼ cup unsweetened cocoa powder
    ⅓ cup peanut butter-flavored chips, chopped
    ¼ cup all-purpose flour
    ⅓ cup miniature chocolate chips

**1.** Remove each dough from wrapper according to package directions.

**2.** Place sugar cookie dough and cocoa in large bowl; mix with fork to blend. Stir in peanut butter chips.

**3.** Place peanut butter cookie dough and flour in another large bowl; mix with fork to blend. Stir in chocolate chips. Divide each dough in half; cover and refrigerate 1 hour.

**4.** Roll each dough on floured surface to 12×6-inch rectangle. Layer each half of peanut butter dough onto each half of chocolate dough. Roll up doughs, starting at long end to form 2 (12-inch) rolls. Wrap in plastic wrap; refrigerate 1 hour.

**5.** Preheat oven to 375°F. Cut dough into ½-inch-thick slices. Place cookies 2 inches apart on ungreased cookie sheets.

**6.** Bake 10 to 12 minutes or until lightly browned. Remove to wire racks; cool completely.

*Makes 4 dozen cookies*

# Choco-Scutterbotch

⅔ **Butter Flavor CRISCO® Stick or ⅔ cup Butter Flavor CRISCO® all-vegetable shortening**

½ **cup firmly packed light brown sugar**

**2 eggs**

**1 package (18¼ ounces) deluxe yellow cake mix**

**1 cup toasted rice cereal**

½ **cup butterscotch chips**

½ **cup milk chocolate chunks**

½ **cup semisweet chocolate chips**

½ **cup coarsely chopped walnuts or pecans**

**1.** Heat oven to 375°F. Place sheets of foil on countertop for cooling cookies.

**2.** Combine ⅔ cup shortening and brown sugar in large bowl. Beat at medium speed of electric mixer until well blended. Beat in eggs.

**3.** Add cake mix gradually at low speed. Mix until well blended. Stir in cereal, butterscotch chips, chocolate chunks, chocolate chips and nuts. Stir until well blended.

**4.** Shape dough into 1¼-inch balls. Place 2 inches apart on ungreased baking sheet. Flatten slightly. Shape sides to form circle, if necessary.

**5.** Bake for 7 to 9 minutes or until lightly browned around edges. *Do not overbake.* Cool 2 minutes on baking sheet. Remove cookies to foil to cool completely.          *Makes 3 dozen cookies*

# Moons and Stars

**1 cup butter, softened**

**1 cup sugar**

**1 egg**

**2 teaspoons lemon peel**

**½ teaspoon almond extract**

**3 cups all-purpose flour**

**½ cup ground almonds**

**Assorted colored icings, hard candies and colored sprinkles**

**1.** Preheat oven to 350°F. Grease cookie sheets.

**2.** Beat butter, sugar, egg, lemon peel and almond extract in large bowl at medium speed of electric mixer until light and fluffy.

**3.** Combine flour and almonds in medium bowl. Add flour mixture to butter mixture; stir just until combined.

**4.** Roll dough on lightly floured surface to ⅛- to ¼-inch thickness. Cut out cookies using moon and star cookie cutters. Place cookies 2 inches apart on prepared cookie sheets.

**5.** Bake 7 to 9 minutes or until set but not browned. Cool on cookie sheets 2 minutes. Remove to wire racks; cool completely.

**6.** Decorate cookies with icings, candies and sprinkles as desired.

*Makes about 4 dozen cookies*

# Butterfly Cookies

2¼ **cups all-purpose flour**

¼ **teaspoon salt**

1 **cup sugar**

¾ **cup (1½ sticks) butter, softened**

1 **egg**

1 **teaspoon vanilla**

1 **teaspoon almond extract**

**White frosting, assorted food colorings, colored sugars, assorted small decors, gummy fruit and hard candies for decoration**

**1.** Combine flour and salt in medium bowl; set aside.

**2.** Beat sugar and butter in large bowl at medium speed of electric mixer until fluffy. Beat in egg, vanilla and almond extract. Gradually add flour mixture. Beat at low speed until well blended. Divide dough in half. Cover; refrigerate 30 minutes or until firm.

**3.** Preheat oven to 350°F. Grease cookie sheets. Roll half of dough on lightly floured surface to ¼-inch thickness. Cut out cookies using butterfly cookie cutters. Repeat with remaining dough.

**4.** Bake 12 to 15 minutes or until edges are lightly browned. Remove to wire racks; cool completely.

**5.** Tint portions of white frosting with assorted food colorings. Spread desired colors of frosting over cookies. Decorate as desired.

*Makes about 20 to 22 cookies*

# Hershey's Milk Chocolate Chip Giant Cookies

6 tablespoons butter, softened

½ cup granulated sugar

¼ cup packed light brown sugar

½ teaspoon vanilla extract

1 egg

1 cup all-purpose flour

½ teaspoon baking soda

2 cups (11½-ounce package) HERSHEY'S Milk Chocolate Chips

Frosting (optional)

Ice cream (optional)

**1.** Heat oven to 350°F. Line two 9-inch round baking pans with foil, extending foil over edges of pans.

**2.** Beat butter, granulated sugar, brown sugar and vanilla until fluffy. Add egg; beat well. Stir together flour and baking soda; gradually add to butter mixture, beating until well blended. Stir in milk chocolate chips. Spread one half of batter into each prepared pan, spreading to 1 inch from edge. (Cookies will spread to edge when baking.)

**3.** Bake 18 to 22 minutes or until lightly browned. Cool completely; carefully lift cookies from pans and remove foil. Frost, if desired. Cut each cookie into wedges; serve topped with scoop of ice cream, if desired. *Makes about 12 to 16 servings*

**Tip:** Bake cookies on the middle rack of the oven, one pan at a time. Uneven browning can occur if baking on more than one rack at the same time.

# Honey Bees

¾ **cup shortening**

½ **cup sugar**

¼ **cup honey**

 1 **egg**

½ **teaspoon vanilla**

 2 **cups all-purpose flour**

⅓ **cup cornmeal**

 1 **teaspoon baking powder**

½ **teaspoon salt**

   **Yellow and black icings or gels and gummy fruit**

**1.** Beat shortening, sugar and honey in large bowl at medium speed of electric mixer until fluffy. Add egg and vanilla; mix until well blended. Combine flour, cornmeal, baking powder and salt in medium bowl. Add to shortening mixture; mix at low speed until well blended. Shape dough into disc. Wrap in plastic wrap; refrigerate 2 hours or overnight.

**2.** Preheat oven to 375°F. Divide dough into 24 equal sections. Shape each section into oval-shaped ball. Place 2 inches apart on ungreased cookie sheets.

**3.** Bake 10 to 12 minutes or until lightly browned. Cool 2 minutes on cookie sheets. Remove to wire racks; cool completely.

**4.** Decorate cookies with yellow and black icings, gummy fruit and decors to resemble honey bees.

*Makes 2 dozen cookies*

# Kaleidoscope Cookies

**1 package (20 ounces) refrigerated sugar cookie dough**
**All-purpose flour (optional)**
**Blue and red liquid food colorings**
**2 tablespoons sprinkles, multi-colored coarse sugar or rock sugar, divided**

**1.** Remove dough from wrapper according to package directions. Cut dough into 5 equal sections. Cover and refrigerate 1 section. Sprinkle remaining 4 sections with flour to minimize sticking, if necessary.

**2.** Add blue food coloring to 1 section in medium bowl; mix using wooden spoon until well blended. Repeat with another section of dough and red food coloring. Shape each section into 7½-inch log. Cover and refrigerate.

**3.** Add 1 tablespoon sprinkles to third section in medium bowl; mix using wooden spoon until well blended. Repeat with fourth section of dough and remaining 1 tablespoon sprinkles. Shape each section into 7½-inch log. Cover and refrigerate.

**4.** Roll out reserved section of plain dough on sheet of waxed paper to 7½×8½-inch rectangle. Place blue dough log and 1 sprinkled dough log in middle of rectangle. Place remaining sprinkled dough log on top of blue dough log and pink dough log on top of first sprinkled dough log.

**5.** Bring waxed paper and closest edge of dough up and over tops of logs. Press gently. Repeat with opposite side, overlapping dough edges. Press gently. Wrap waxed paper around dough and twist ends to secure.

**6.** Freeze 20 minutes. Preheat oven to 350°F. Grease cookie sheets.

**7.** Remove waxed paper. Cut log with sharp knife into ½-inch slices. Place 2 inches apart on prepared cookie sheets.

**8.** Bake 15 to 17 minutes or until edges are lightly browned. Remove to wire racks; cool completely.

*Makes about 15 cookies*

# Our House

**1 package (18 ounces) refrigerated cookie dough, any flavor**

**All-purpose flour (optional)**

**Blue, green, white and purple icings, granulated sugar, yellow-colored sugar, green gumdrops, red licorice, small decors and hard candies**

**1.** Preheat oven to 350°F. Line large cookie sheet with parchment paper.

**2.** Remove dough from wrapper according to package directions. Roll small piece of dough into 1½-inch square; reserve.

**3.** Press remaining dough into 12×9-inch rectangle on prepared cookie sheet. Sprinkle with flour to minimize sticking, if necessary.

**4.** Place reserved dough at top of rectangle to make chimney. Press to seal.

**5.** Bake 10 to 12 minutes or until edges are lightly browned. Cool on baking sheet 5 minutes. Slide house and parchment paper onto wire rack; cool completely.

**6.** Decorate as shown in photo. Use flat decorating tip for clapboards and shingles, yellow colored sugar for windows, star decorating tip for columns and steps and gumdrops for bushes.

*Makes 1 cookie house*

**Tip:** This is a perfect rainy-day project. Keep your kids entertained by decorating this cookie house as directed or let their minds go wild and decorate it however they like.

# Shapers

**2 packages (20 ounces each) refrigerated sugar cookie dough**
**Red, yellow, green and blue paste food colorings**
**1 container (16 ounces) vanilla frosting**

**1.** Remove dough from wrapper according to package directions. Cut each roll of dough in half.

**2.** Beat ¼ of dough and red food coloring in medium bowl until well blended. Shape red dough into 5-inch log on sheet of waxed paper; set aside.

**3.** Repeat with remaining dough and food colorings. Cover; refrigerate tinted logs 1 hour or until firm.

**4.** Roll or shape each log on smooth surface to create circular, triangular, square and oval-shaped logs. Use ruler to keep triangle and square sides flat. Cover; refrigerate dough 1 hour or until firm.

**5.** Preheat oven to 350°F. Cut shaped dough into ¼-inch slices. Place 2 inches apart on ungreased baking sheets. Bake 9 to 12 minutes. Remove to wire racks; cool completely.

**6.** Spoon frosting into resealable plastic food storage bag; seal. Cut tiny tip from corner of bag. Pipe frosting around each cookie to define shape.          *Makes about 6½ dozen cookies*

**Tip:** If you have extra liquid food colorings at home, tint the vanilla frosting different colors. Frost cookies using contrasting colored frosting, for example green frosting on a red cookie.

# Myrtle the Turtle

¾ **cup (1½ sticks) unsalted butter, softened**

¼ **cup granulated sugar**

¼ **cup packed light brown sugar**

1 **egg yolk**

1¾ **cups all-purpose flour**

¾ **teaspoon baking powder**

⅛ **teaspoon salt**

   **Green food coloring**

   **Assorted colored hard candies, crushed**

   **Assorted colored icings, small candies and decors**

**1.** Combine butter, granulated sugar, brown sugar and egg yolk in medium bowl until well blended. Add flour, baking powder and salt; mix until well blended. Tint dough with food coloring to desired shade of green; shape dough into disc. Wrap in plastic wrap and refrigerate about 1 hour.

**2.** Preheat oven to 350°F. Line cookie sheets with foil; lightly grease foil. Roll dough on lightly floured surface to ¼-inch thickness. For turtle shells, cut out dough with 4-inch round cookie cutter; cut rounds in half. Place shells 2 inches apart on prepared cookie sheets. Using hors d'oeuvre cutters, miniature cookie cutters or knife, cut out shapes in decorative pattern from shells.

**3.** Cut portion of remaining dough into 1-inch circle for heads. Moisten back of dough head and place at bottom center of shell; press down. Cut remaining dough into ½- to ¾-inch circles; cut circles in half for feet. Place feet on prepared cookie sheet near left and right edges of shells; press dough edges of feet and shells together gently to seal. Decorate faces with candies as desired, or leave plain to decorate after baking. Generously fill cutout shapes in shells with crushed candies.

**4.** Bake 8 to 10 minutes or until edges are lightly browned and candy is melted. Transfer foil and cookies to wire racks; let cool completely. Decorate faces and shells with assorted icings, candies and decors as desired.

*Makes 1 dozen cookies*

**Tip:** To crush hard candies, unwrap candies and separate into colors. Place each color in separate heavy resealable plastic food storage bag. Crush candies with rolling pin or hammer.

**36** Bake Sale Bounty

# Smushy Cookies

**1 package (20 ounces) refrigerated cookie dough, any flavor**
**All-purpose flour (optional)**

**Fillings**

**Peanut butter, multi-colored miniature marshmallows, assorted colored sprinkles, chocolate-covered raisins and caramel candy squares**

**1.** Preheat oven to 350°F. Grease cookie sheets.

**2.** Remove dough from wrapper according to package directions. Cut into 4 equal sections. Reserve 1 section; refrigerate remaining 3 sections.

**3.** Roll reserved dough to ¼-inch thickness. Sprinkle with flour to minimize sticking, if necessary. Cut out cookies using 2½-inch round cookie cutter. Transfer to prepared cookie sheets. Repeat with remaining dough, working with 1 section at a time.

**4.** Bake 8 to 11 minutes or until edges are light golden brown. Remove to wire racks; cool completely.

**5.** To make sandwich, spread about 1½ tablespoons peanut butter on underside of 1 cookie to within ¼ inch of edge. Sprinkle with miniature marshmallows and candy pieces. Top with second cookie, pressing gently. Repeat with remaining cookies and fillings.

**6.** Just before serving, place sandwiches on paper towels. Microwave at HIGH 15 to 25 seconds or until fillings become soft. *Makes about 8 to 10 sandwich cookies*

**Tip:** Invite the neighbor kids over on a rainy day to make these fun Smushy Cookies. Be sure to have lots of filling choices available so each child can create their own unique cookies.

# Domino Cookies

**1 package (20 ounces) refrigerated sugar cookie dough**
**All-purpose flour (optional)**
**½ cup semisweet chocolate chips**

**1.** Preheat oven to 350°F. Grease cookie sheets.

**2.** Remove dough from wrapper according to package directions. Cut dough into 4 equal sections. Reserve 1 section; refrigerate remaining 3 sections.

**3.** Roll reserved dough to ⅛-inch thickness. Sprinkle with flour to minimize sticking, if necessary. Cut out 9 (2½×1¾-inch) rectangles using sharp knife. Place 2 inches apart on prepared cookie sheets.

**4.** Score each cookie across middle with sharp knife. Gently press chocolate chips, point side down, into dough to resemble various dominos. Repeat with remaining dough, scraps and chocolate chips.

**5.** Bake 8 to 10 minutes or until edges are light golden brown. Remove to wire racks; cool completely. *Makes 3 dozen cookies*

**Tip:** Use these adorable cookies as a learning tool for kids. They can count the number of chocolate chips in each cookie and arrange them in lots of ways: highest to lowest, numerically or even solve simple math problems. As a treat, they can eat the cookies afterwards.

# Pretty Posies

1 package (20 ounces) refrigerated sugar cookie dough

Orange and purple food colorings

1 tablespoon sprinkles

All-purpose flour (optional)

**1.** Remove dough from wrapper. Reserve ⅙ of dough. Add orange food coloring and sprinkles to reserved dough until well blended; shape into 7½ inch log. Wrap with plastic wrap and refrigerate 30 minutes or until firm. Add purple food coloring to remaining dough until well blended. Shape dough into disc. Wrap with plastic wrap and refrigerate 30 minutes or until firm.

**2.** Roll out purple dough to 6×7½-inch rectangle on sheet of waxed paper. Place orange log in center of rectangle. Bring waxed paper and edges of purple dough up and over top of orange log; press gently. Overlap purple dough edges slightly; press gently. Wrap waxed paper around dough and twist ends to secure. Freeze log 20 minutes.

**3.** Preheat oven to 350°F. Lightly grease cookie sheets. Remove waxed paper from dough log. Cut log into ¼-inch slices. Place 2 inches apart on prepared cookie sheets. Using 2½-inch flower-shaped cookie cutter, cut slices into flowers; remove and discard dough scraps.

**4.** Bake 15 to 17 minutes or until edges are lightly browned. Remove to wire racks; cool completely.

*Makes about 1½ dozen cookies*

# Lady Bugs

¾ **cup shortening**

½ **cup sugar**

¼ **cup honey**

 1 **egg**

½ **teaspoon vanilla**

 2 **cups all-purpose flour**

⅓ **cup cornmeal**

 1 **teaspoon baking powder**

½ **teaspoon salt**

   **Orange and black icings and yellow candy-coated chocolate pieces**

**1.** Beat shortening, sugar and honey in large bowl at medium speed with electric mixer until light and fluffy. Add egg and vanilla; mix until well blended. Combine flour, cornmeal, baking powder and salt in medium bowl. Add to shortening mixture; mix at low speed until blended. Shape dough into disc. Wrap in plastic wrap and chill 2 hours or overnight.

**2.** Preheat oven to 375°F. Divide dough into 24 equal sections. Shape each section into 2×1¼-inch oval-shaped ball. Place balls 2 inches apart on ungreased cookie sheets.

**3.** Bake 10 to 12 minutes or until lightly browned. Cool on cookie sheets 2 minutes. Remove to wire racks; cool completely.

**4.** Decorate cookies with orange and black icings and candy-coated pieces to resemble lady bugs.

*Makes 2 dozen cookies*

**44** Bake Sale Bounty

# Musical Instrument Cookies

**1 package (18 ounces) refrigerated sugar cookie dough**
**All-purpose flour (optional)**
**Assorted colored frostings, colored gels, colored sugars, candy and small decors**

**1.** Preheat oven to 350°F. Grease cookie sheets.

**2.** Remove dough from wrapper according to package directions. Divide dough into 2 equal sections. Reserve 1 section; cover and refrigerate remaining section.

**3.** Roll reserved dough on lightly floured surface to ¼-inch thickness. Sprinkle with flour to minimize sticking, if necessary. Cut out cookies using about 3½-inch musical notes and instrument cookie cutters. Place cookies 2 inches apart on prepared cookie sheets. Repeat with remaining dough.

**4.** Bake 10 to 12 minutes or until edges are lightly browned. Remove from oven. Cool on cookie sheets 2 minutes. Remove to wire racks; cool completely.

**5.** Decorate with colored frostings, gels, sugars and assorted decors as shown in photo.

*Makes about 2 dozen cookies*

# "Blondie" Brownies

½ Butter Flavor CRISCO® Stick or ½ cup Butter Flavor CRISCO® all-vegetable shortening
   plus additional for greasing

1 tablespoon milk

1 cup firmly packed brown sugar

1 egg

1 cup all-purpose flour

½ teaspoon baking powder

⅛ teaspoon salt

1 teaspoon vanilla

½ cup chopped walnuts

**1.** Heat oven to 350°F. Grease 8×8×2-inch pan with shortening. Place cooling rack on countertop.

**2.** Combine ½ cup shortening and milk in large microwave-safe bowl. Microwave at 50% (MEDIUM). Stir after 1 minute. Repeat until melted (or melt on rangetop in large saucepan on low heat). Stir in sugar. Stir in egg quickly. Combine flour, baking powder and salt. Stir into sugar mixture. Stir in vanilla and nuts. Spread in prepared pan.

**3.** Bake at 350°F for 27 to 30 minutes, or until toothpick inserted in center comes out clean. *Do not overbake.* Cool in pan on cooling rack. Cut into 2×2-inch squares.          *Makes 16 squares*

# Checkerboard Cookie

¾ cup (1½ sticks) butter, softened

1 cup sugar

2 eggs

1 teaspoon vanilla

2¾ cups self-rising flour

   All-purpose flour

   Red and black icings

**1.** Beat butter and sugar in large bowl at high speed of electric mixer until light and fluffy. Add eggs and vanilla; stir to combine. Add self-rising flour; stir until just combined. Cover and refrigerate 30 minutes.

**2.** Preheat oven to 350°F. Grease cookie sheets.

**3.** Roll ¼ of dough on lightly floured surface to ¼-inch thickness. Cut 24 circles with 1-inch round cookie cutter. Place on prepared cookie sheets.

**4.** Bake 8 to 10 minutes or until cookies turn light golden brown. Cool on cookie sheet 2 minutes. Remove to wire rack; cool completely.

**5.** Combine scraps of dough with remaining dough. Roll on lightly floured surface to 12-inch square. Place on greased 15½×12-inch cookie sheet.

**6.** Bake 10 to 12 minutes or until middle does not leave indentation when lightly touched with fingertips. Cool on cookie sheet 5 minutes. Slide checkerboard onto wire rack; cool completely.

**7.** Divide surface of checkerboard into 8 equal rows containing 8 equal columns. Alternate every other square with red and black icing to create checkerboard. Spread red icing on 12 checker playing pieces and black on remaining 12 checker playing pieces. Allow pieces to stand until icing is set. Place red pieces on black squares and black pieces on red squares.

*Makes 1 checkerboard cookie*

# Baseball Caps

**1 cup butter, softened**

**7 ounces almond paste**

**¾ cup sugar**

**1 egg**

**1 teaspoon vanilla**

**¼ teaspoon salt**

**3 cups all-purpose flour**

**Assorted colored icings and colored candies**

**1.** Preheat oven to 350°F. Grease cookie sheets. Beat butter, almond paste, sugar, egg, vanilla and salt in large bowl at high speed of electric mixer until light and fluffy. Add flour all at once; stir just to combine.

**2.** Roll ¼ of dough on lightly floured surface to ⅛-inch thickness. Cut out 1-inch circles. Place cutouts 2 inches apart on prepared cookie sheets.

**3.** Shape remaining dough into 1-inch balls.* Place one ball on top of half dough circle so about ½ inch of circle sticks out to form bill of baseball cap. Repeat with remaining dough balls and circles.

**4.** Bake 10 to 12 minutes or until lightly browned. If bills brown too quickly, cut small strips of foil and cover with shiny side of foil facing up. Let cool on cookie sheets 2 minutes. Remove to wire racks; cool completely. Decorate with icings and candies as desired.

*Makes about 3 dozen cookies*

*Use a 1-tablespoon scoop to keep the baseball caps uniform in size and professional looking.*

# Holiday Delights

## Caramel Corn Apple-O's

7 cups popped butter-flavor microwave popcorn

2¼ cups apple cinnamon cereal rings

½ cup chopped dried apples or apricots

¼ cup chopped nuts, optional

1 package (14 ounces) caramels, unwrapped

1 to 2 tablespoons water*

2 tablespoons butter or margarine

   Long cinnamon sticks or wooden craft sticks (optional)

*Start with 1 tablespoon water and add more if needed for consistency. Fresher caramels will require less water.

**1.** Combine popcorn, cereal, apples and nuts, if desired, in large bowl.

**2.** Microwave caramels, water and butter at HIGH 2½ to 3 minutes, stirring at one minute intervals until melted and smooth.

**3.** Pour caramel over popcorn mixture, tossing with buttered wooden spoon to coat. Let set until just slightly warm.

**4.** Dampen hands and shape mixture into 8 balls. Shape balls around sticks, if desired. Place on lightly buttered waxed paper until ready to serve. *Makes 8 balls*

52

## Cookie Gobblers

**8 marshmallow puff cookies**

**4 striped shortbread ring cookies**

**¼ cup semisweet chocolate chips, melted**

**8 pieces candy corn**

### Supplies

**8 (2½×1½-inch) pieces lightweight cardboard (optional)**

**1.** Cut down into marshmallow cookie halfway between center and edge. Starting in back, cut horizontally toward first cut. Dip knife in hot water and dry it before each cut. Discard pieces.

**2.** Cut striped cookies in half. Attach 1 striped cookie half with melted chocolate to cut edge of marshmallow cookie to form tail. Attach candy corn to front of turkey with melted chocolate as shown. Repeat with remaining cookies.

**3.** To make place cards, write names near top edges of cardboard. Place behind striped cookie half; attach with melted chocolate, if desired. *Makes 8 place cards*

## Give Thanks Cornucopias

**8 ice cream sugar cones**

**3 ounces semisweet chocolate, melted**

**Assorted fall candies**

### Supplies

**8 (2×¾-inch) pieces lightweight cardboard (optional)**

**1.** Dip edges of cones into melted chocolate; let stand on wire racks or waxed paper until chocolate is firm. Place each cone on its side; fill with candy.

**2.** To make place cards, write names on pieces of cardboard. Attach to tops of cones with melted chocolate. *Makes 8 favors or place cards*

Left to right: Cookie Gobblers,
Give Thanks Cornucopias

# Festive Easter Cookies

1 cup (2 sticks) butter, softened

2 cups powdered sugar

1 egg

2 teaspoons grated lemon peel

1 teaspoon vanilla

3 cups all-purpose flour

½ teaspoon salt

Royal Icing (recipe follows)

Assorted food colorings

Assorted sprinkles and candies

**1.** Beat butter and powdered sugar in large bowl at high speed of electric mixer until fluffy. Add egg, lemon peel and vanilla; mix well. Combine flour and salt in medium bowl. Add to butter mixture; mix well.

**2.** Divide dough in half. Wrap each half with plastic wrap. Refrigerate 3 hours or overnight.

**3.** Preheat oven to 375°F. Roll dough on floured surface to ⅛-inch thickness. Cut out dough using Easter cookie cutters, such as eggs, bunnies and tulips. Place cutouts on ungreased cookie sheets.

**4.** Bake 8 to 12 minutes or just until edges are very lightly browned. Remove to wire racks; cool completely. Prepare Royal Icing; tint with food colorings as desired. Decorate with sprinkles and candies. *Makes 4 dozen cookies*

## Royal Icing

1 egg white,* at room temperature

2 to 2½ cups sifted powdered sugar

½ teaspoon almond extract

*Use only grade A clean, uncracked egg.*

**1.** Beat egg white in small bowl with electric mixer at high speed until foamy.

**2.** Gradually add 2 cups powdered sugar and almond extract. Beat at low speed until moistened. Increase mixer speed to high and beat until icing is stiff, adding additional powdered sugar if needed.

# Yuletide Twisters

**1 (6-ounce) package premier white baking bars**

**4 teaspoons fat-free (skim) milk**

**4 teaspoons light corn syrup**

**8 ounces reduced-salt pretzel twists (about 80)**

   **Cookie decorations, colored sugar or chocolate sprinkles**

**1.** Line baking sheet with waxed paper; set aside.

**2.** Melt baking bars in small saucepan over low heat, stirring constantly. Stir in skim milk and corn syrup. Do not remove saucepan from heat.

**3.** Holding pretzel with fork, dip 1 side of each pretzel into melted mixture to coat. Place, coated side up, on prepared baking sheet; immediately sprinkle with desired decorations. Refrigerate until firm, 15 to 20 minutes.

*Makes 10 servings*

**Chocolate Twisters:** Substitute semisweet chocolate chips for premier white baking bars.

**Caramel Dippity Do's:** Heat 1 cup nonfat caramel sauce and ⅓ cup finely chopped pecans in small saucepan until warm. Pour into small serving bowl. Serve with pretzels for dipping. Makes 8 servings (about 2 tablespoons each).

**Chocolate Dippity Do's:** Heat 1 cup nonfat hot fudge sauce and ⅓ cup finely chopped pecans or walnuts in small saucepan until warm. Pour into small serving bowl. Serve with pretzels for dipping. Makes 8 servings (about 2 tablespoons each).

## Jack-O'-Lantern Chili Cups

**2 cans (11.5 ounces each) refrigerated corn breadstick dough (8 breadsticks each)** *or*
**3 cans (4.5 ounces each) refrigerated buttermilk biscuits (6 biscuits each)**

**1 can (15 ounces) mild chili with beans**

**1 cup frozen corn**

**6 slices Cheddar cheese**

**Olive slices, bell pepper and carrot pieces for decoration**

**1.** Preheat oven to 425°F. Lightly grease 16 to 18 regular-size (2½-inch) muffin pan cups. Lightly roll out corn bread dough to press together perforations. Cut out 18 circles with 3-inch round cookie cutter. Press 1 circle onto bottom and 1 inch up side of each muffin cup.

**2.** Combine chili and corn in medium bowl. Fill each muffin cup with 1 tablespoon chili. Cut out 16 to 18 circles from cheese with 2 inch round cookie cutter; place rounds over chili mixture in cups. Decorate cheese with olive, bell pepper and carrot pieces to resemble jack-o'-lanterns. Bake 10 to 12 minutes or until corn bread is completely baked and cheese is melted.

*Makes about 8 servings*

## Cranberry Gorp

¼ **cup unsalted butter**

¼ **cup packed light brown sugar**

1 **tablespoon maple syrup**

1 **teaspoon curry powder**

½ **teaspoon ground cinnamon**

1½ **cups dried cranberries**

1½ **cups coarsely chopped walnuts and/or slivered almonds**

1½ **cups lightly salted pretzel nuggets**

**1.** Preheat oven to 300°F. Grease 15×10-inch jelly-roll pan. Combine butter, brown sugar and maple syrup in large saucepan; heat over medium heat until butter is melted. Stir in curry powder and cinnamon. Add cranberries, walnuts and pretzels; stir to combine.

**2.** Spread mixture on prepared pan. Bake 15 minutes or until mixture is crunchy and light brown.

*Makes 20 servings*

## Yuletide Linzer Bars

1⅓ cups butter, softened
¾ cup sugar
1 egg
1 teaspoon grated lemon peel
2½ cups all-purpose flour
1½ cups whole almonds, ground
1 teaspoon ground cinnamon
¾ cup raspberry preserves
Powdered sugar

Preheat oven to 350°F. Grease 13×9-inch baking pan.

Beat butter and sugar in large bowl at medium speed of electric mixer until creamy. Beat in egg and lemon peel until blended. Mix in flour, almonds and cinnamon until well blended.

Press 2 cups dough onto bottom of prepared pan. Spread preserves over crust. Press remaining dough, a small amount at a time, evenly over preserves.

Bake 35 to 40 minutes until golden brown. Cool in pan on wire rack. Sprinkle with powdered sugar; cut into bars.

*Makes 36 bars*

## Jack-O-Lantern Snacks

**8 ounces cream cheese, softened**
**Red and yellow food coloring**
**8 large slices dark pumpernickel bread**
**1 small green bell pepper**
**Sliced Genoa salami**

**1.** Place cream cheese in a small bowl. Add 8 drops red and 6 drops yellow food coloring to turn the cream cheese orange. Mix well and adjust color as desired.

**2.** Toast bread and allow to cool. Using a large pumpkin cookie cutter or metal 1-cup measure, cut a round shape from each slice of toast leaving a "stem" on top. Spread cream cheese over toast all the way to edges. Cut "stems" from green pepper and place over stem on toast. Cut triangle "eyes" and a mouth with several "teeth" from sliced salami. Arrange over each pumpkin toast. *Makes 8 servings*

## Festive Popcorn Treats

**6 cups popped popcorn**
**½ cup sugar**
**½ cup light corn syrup**
**¼ cup peanut butter**
**Green food coloring**
**¼ cup red cinnamon candies**

Line baking sheet with waxed paper. Pour popcorn into large bowl. Combine sugar and corn syrup in medium saucepan. Bring to a boil over medium heat, stirring constantly; boil 1 minute. Remove from heat. Add peanut butter and green food coloring; stir until peanut butter is completely melted. Pour over popcorn; stir to coat well. Lightly butter hands and shape popcorn mixture into trees. While trees are still warm, press red cinnamon candies into trees. Place on prepared baking sheet; let stand until firm, about 30 minutes. *Makes 6 servings*

# Chocolate Bunny Cookies

**1 (21-ounce) package DUNCAN HINES® Family-Style Chewy Fudge Brownie Mix**

**1 egg**

**¼ cup water**

**¼ cup vegetable oil**

**1⅓ cups pecan halves (96)**

**1 container DUNCAN HINES® Creamy Home-Style Dark Chocolate Fudge Frosting**

**White chocolate chips**

**1.** Preheat oven to 350°F. Grease baking sheets.

**2.** Combine brownie mix, egg, water and oil in large bowl. Stir with spoon until well blended, about 50 strokes. Drop by level tablespoonfuls 2 inches apart on greased baking sheets. Place two pecan halves, flat-side up, on each cookie for ears. Bake at 350°F for 10 to 12 minutes or until set. Cool 2 minutes on baking sheets. Remove to cooling racks. Cool completely.

**3.** Spread Dark Chocolate Fudge frosting on one cookie. Place white chocolate chips, upside down, on frosting for eyes and nose. Dot each eye with frosting using toothpick. Repeat for remaining cookies. Allow frosting to set before storing cookies between layers of waxed paper in airtight container.                                              *Makes 4 dozen cookies*

**Tip:** For variety, frost cookies with Duncan Hines® Vanilla Frosting and use semisweet chocolate chips for the eyes and noses.

## Chocolate Spiders

¼ cup butter

1 package (12 ounces) semisweet chocolate chips

1 cup butterscotch-flavored chips

¼ cup creamy peanut butter

4 cups crisp rice cereal

Chow mein noodles and assorted candies

1. Line baking sheet with waxed paper.

2. Combine butter, chocolate chips and butterscotch chips in large saucepan; stir over medium heat until chips are melted and mixture is well blended. Remove from heat. Add peanut butter; mix well. Add cereal; stir to evenly coat.

3. Drop mixture by tablespoonfuls, onto prepared baking sheet; insert chow mein noodles for legs and add candies for eyes.                                    *Makes about 3 dozen*

**Doughnut Hole Spiders:** Substitute chocolate-covered doughnut holes for shaped cereal mixture. Insert black string licorice, cut into 1½-inch lengths, into doughnut holes for legs. Use desired color decorating icing to dot onto doughnut holes for eyes.

## Quick Candy Ornaments

**Ingredients**

1 package (7.5 ounces) hard candies, assorted colors

4 to 6 (2- or 3-inch) ovenproof open-topped cookie cutters

**Supplies**

Clear nylon thread

1. Unwrap candies. Separate into colors; place each color in separate heavy resealable plastic food storage bag. Crush candies with rolling pin or hammer.

**2.** Line baking sheet with foil; spray with nonstick cooking spray. Cut 6 pieces of foil, each about 8 inches square; fold each piece in half.

**3.** Place 1 cookie cutter in center of each piece of doubled foil; bring sides of foil up around cookie cutter, keeping foil in center as flat as possible. Press foil tightly to all sides of cutters. Place on prepared baking sheet, open tops facing up.

**4.** Preheat oven to 400°F. Spoon crushed candies into cookie cutters to a depth of about ½ inch. Bake 8 to 10 minutes or until candy is melted. Meanwhile, cut thread into 6 (8-inch) lengths; bring ends of thread together and tie in knots. Remove ornaments from oven. While candy is warm, soft and still in cutter, place knotted end of thread near top of each shape for hanging; press into ornament with handle of wooden spoon. Cool completely.

**5.** Peel foil off ornaments. Gently bend cutters to loosen ornaments. Break or scrape off ragged edges of ornaments with small knife. *Makes 4 to 6 ornaments*

# Old-Fashioned Pop Corn Balls

**2 quarts popped JOLLY TIME® Pop Corn**

**1 cup sugar**

**⅓ cup light or dark corn syrup**

**⅓ cup water**

**¼ cup butter or margarine**

**½ teaspoon salt**

**1 teaspoon vanilla**

Keep popped pop corn warm in 200°F oven while preparing syrup. In 2-quart saucepan, stir together sugar, corn syrup, water, butter and salt. Cook over medium heat, stirring constantly, until mixture comes to a boil. Continue cooking without stirring until temperature reaches 270°F on candy thermometer or until small amount of syrup dropped into very cold water separates into threads which are hard but not brittle. Remove from heat. Add vanilla; stir just enough to mix through hot syrup. Slowly pour over popped pop corn, stirring to coat well. Cool just enough to handle. With JOLLY TIME® Pop Corn Ball Maker or buttered hands, shape into balls.

*Makes 12 medium-sized pop corn balls*

# Chip-a-licious

## Caramel Lace Chocolate Chip Cookies

¼ **Butter Flavor CRISCO® Stick or ¼ cup Butter Flavor CRISCO® all-vegetable shortening plus additional for greasing**

½ **cup light corn syrup**

1 **tablespoon brown sugar**

1½ **teaspoons grated orange peel (optional)**

½ **teaspoon vanilla**

½ **cup all-purpose flour**

¼ **teaspoon salt**

⅓ **cup semisweet chocolate chips**

⅓ **cup coarsely chopped pecans**

**1.** Heat oven to 375°F. Grease baking sheets with shortening.

**2.** Combine ¼ cup shortening, corn syrup, brown sugar, orange peel and vanilla in large bowl. Beat at medium speed of electric mixer until well blended.

**3.** Combine flour and salt. Mix into creamed mixture at low speed until blended. Stir in chocolate chips and nuts. Drop teaspoonfuls of dough 4 inches apart onto prepared baking sheets.

**4.** Bake one baking sheet at a time at 375°F for 5 minutes or until edges are golden brown. (Chips and nuts will remain in center while dough spreads out.) *Do not overbake.* Cool 2 minutes on baking sheets. Lift each cookie edge with spatula. Grasp cookie edge gently and lightly pinch or flute edge, bringing it up to chips and nuts in center. Work around each cookie until completely fluted. Remove to cooling rack.                *Makes about 3 dozen cookies*

Caramel Lace Chocolate
Chip Cookies

6 + 7 = 13    2 + 4 = 6    8 + 3 = 11

# Walnut-Orange Chocolate Chippers

1½ cups all-purpose flour

½ cup packed brown sugar

½ cup granulated sugar

1½ teaspoons baking powder

½ teaspoon salt

⅓ cup butter, softened

2 eggs, slightly beaten

2 cups (12 ounces) semisweet chocolate chips

1 cup coarsely chopped California walnuts

2 tablespoons grated orange rind

Combine flour, brown sugar, granulated sugar, baking powder and salt in large bowl; mix in butter and eggs. Add remaining ingredients and mix thoroughly (batter will be stiff). Drop tablespoonfuls of dough 2 inches apart onto ungreased cookies sheets. Bake in preheated 350°F oven 9 to 11 minutes or until lightly browned. Cool 1 minute on cookie sheets; transfer to wire racks to cool completely.

*Makes about 3½ dozen cookies*

**Variation:** Prepare dough as directed above. Spread evenly into greased and floured 9-inch square pan (use wet hands to smooth). Bake at 350°F 25 minutes or until golden brown. Cool; cut into 36 squares.

Favorite recipe from **Walnut Marketing Board**

6 + 7 = 13    2 + 4 = 6    8 + 3 = 11

# Original Nestlé® Toll House® Chocolate Chip Cookies

2¼ cups all-purpose flour

1 teaspoon baking soda

1 teaspoon salt

1 cup (2 sticks) butter or margarine, softened

¾ cup granulated sugar

¾ cup packed brown sugar

1 teaspoon vanilla extract

2 large eggs

2 cups (12-ounce package) NESTLÉ® TOLL HOUSE® Semi-Sweet Chocolate Morsels

1 cup chopped nuts

**PREHEAT** oven to 375°F.

**COMBINE** flour, baking soda and salt in small bowl. Beat butter, granulated sugar, brown sugar and vanilla extract in large mixer bowl until creamy. Add eggs, one at a time, beating well after each addition. Gradually beat in flour mixture. Stir in morsels and nuts. Drop by rounded tablespoon onto ungreased baking sheets.

**BAKE** for 9 to 11 minutes or until golden brown. Cool on baking sheets for 2 minutes; remove to wire racks to cool completely. *Makes about 5 dozen cookies*

**Pan Cookie Variation: GREASE** 15×10-inch jelly-roll pan. Prepare dough as above. Spread into prepared pan. Bake for 20 to 25 minutes or until golden brown. Cool in pan on wire rack. Makes 4 dozen bars.

**Slice and Bake Cookie Variation: PREPARE** dough as above. Divide in half; wrap in wax paper. Refrigerate for 1 hour or until firm. Shape each half into 15-inch log; wrap in wax paper. Refrigerate for 30 minutes. (Dough may be stored in refrigerator for up to 1 week or in freezer for up to 8 weeks.) Preheat oven to 375°F. Cut into ½-inch-thick slices; place on ungreased baking sheets. Bake for 8 to 10 minutes or until golden brown. Cool on baking sheets for 2 minutes; remove to wire racks to cool completely. Makes about 5 dozen cookies. Dough may be stored in refrigerator for up to 1 week or in freezer for up to 8 weeks.

6 + 7 = 13    2 + 4 = 6    8 + 3 = 11

# Peanut Butter Chip Tassies

1 package (3 ounces) cream cheese, softened

½ cup (1 stick) butter, softened

1 cup all-purpose flour

1 egg, slightly beaten

½ cup sugar

2 tablespoons butter, melted

¼ teaspoon lemon juice

¼ teaspoon vanilla extract

1 cup REESE'S® Peanut Butter Chips, chopped*

6 red candied cherries, quartered (optional)

*Do not chop peanut butter chips in food processor or blender.*

**1.** Beat cream cheese and ½ cup butter in medium bowl; stir in flour. Cover; refrigerate about one hour or until dough is firm. Shape into 24 one-inch balls; place each ball into ungreased, small muffin cups (1¾ inches in diameter). Press dough evenly against bottom and sides of each cup.

**2.** Heat oven to 350°F.

**3.** Combine egg, sugar, melted butter, lemon juice and vanilla in medium bowl; stir until smooth. Add chopped peanut butter chips. Fill muffin cups ¾ full with mixture.

**4.** Bake 20 to 25 minutes or until filling is set and lightly browned. Cool completely; remove from pan to wire rack. Garnish with candied cherries, if desired.          *Makes about 2 dozen*

# Ultimate Chocolate Chip Cookies

1¼ cups firmly packed brown sugar

¾ Butter Flavor CRISCO® Stick or ¾ cup Butter Flavor CRISCO® all-vegetable shortening

2 tablespoons milk

1 tablespoon vanilla

1 egg

1¾ cups all-purpose flour

1 teaspoon salt

¾ teaspoon baking soda

1 cup semisweet chocolate chips

1 cup coarsely chopped pecans*

*You can substitute an additional ½ cup semisweet chocolate chips for pecans.

1. Heat oven to 375°F. Place sheets of foil on countertop for cooling cookies.

2. Combine sugar, ¾ cup shortening, milk and vanilla in large bowl. Beat at medium speed of electric mixer until well blended. Beat in egg.

3. Combine flour, salt and baking soda. Mix into shortening mixture at low speed just until blended. Stir in chocolate chips and nuts.

4. Drop by rounded tablespoonfuls 3 inches apart onto ungreased baking sheets.

5. Bake at 375°F for 8 to 10 minutes for chewy cookies or 11 to 13 minutes for crisp cookies. *Do not overbake.* Cool 2 minutes on baking sheets. Remove to foil to cool completely.

*Makes about 3 dozen cookies*

**Drizzle:** Combine 1 teaspoon BUTTER FLAVOR CRISCO® and 1 cup semisweet chocolate chips or 1 cup white melting chocolate, cut into small pieces, in microwave-safe measuring cup. Microwave at 50% (MEDIUM). Stir after 1 minute. Repeat until smooth (or melt on rangetop in small saucepan on very low heat). To thin, add more Butter Flavor Crisco®. Drizzle back and forth over cookies. Sprinkle with nuts before chocolate hardens, if desired. To quickly harden chocolate, place cookies in refrigerator to set.

**Chocolate Dipped:** Melt chocolate as directed for Drizzle. Dip half of cooled cookies in chocolate. Sprinkle with finely chopped nuts before chocolate hardens. Place on waxed paper until chocolate is firm. To quickly harden chocolate, place cookies in refrigerator to set.

**80** Chip-a-licious

6 + 7 = 13    2 + 4 = 6    8 + 3 = 11

# Hershey's "Perfectly Chocolate" Chocolate Chip Cookies

2¼ cups all-purpose flour

⅓ cup HERSHEY'S Cocoa

1 teaspoon baking soda

½ teaspoon salt

1 cup (2 sticks) butter or margarine, softened

¾ cup granulated sugar

¾ cup packed light brown sugar

1 teaspoon vanilla extract

2 eggs

2 cups (12-ounce package) HERSHEY'S Semi-Sweet Chocolate Chips

1 cup chopped nuts (optional)

**1.** Heat oven to 375°F.

**2.** Stir together flour, cocoa, baking soda and salt. Beat butter, granulated sugar, brown sugar and vanilla in large bowl on medium speed of mixer until creamy. Add eggs; beat well. Gradually add flour mixture, beating until well blended. Stir in chocolate chips and nuts, if desired. Drop by rounded teaspoons onto ungreased cookie sheet.

**3.** Bake 8 to 10 minutes or until set. Cool slightly; remove from cookie sheet to wire rack.

*Makes about 5 dozen cookies*

6 + 7 = 13    2 + 4 = 6    8 + 3 = 11

# Chocolate Chip Shells

2 cups all-purpose flour

1⅓ cups (about 8 ounces) NESTLÉ® TOLL HOUSE® Semi-Sweet Chocolate Morsels, *divided*

4 large eggs

1 cup granulated sugar

1 teaspoon orange extract

1 teaspoon vanilla extract

2 tablespoons (about 1 orange) grated orange peel

1 cup (2 sticks) unsalted butter, melted

Sifted powdered sugar

**PREHEAT** oven to 350°F. Generously grease and flour madeleine baking pan(s).

**COMBINE** flour and *1 cup* morsels in medium bowl. Beat eggs, granulated sugar, orange extract, vanilla extract and orange peel in large mixer bowl until light in color. Fold flour mixture and butter alternately into egg mixture, beginning and ending with flour mixture. Spoon heaping tablespoon of batter into each prepared mold.

**BAKE** for 10 to 12 minutes or until wooden pick inserted in center comes out clean. Cool in pan(s) for 1 minute. With tip of knife, release onto wire racks to cool completely. Wash, grease and flour pan(s). Repeat with *remaining* batter.

**SPRINKLE** madeleines very lightly with powdered sugar. Microwave *remaining* morsels in *heavy-duty* resealable plastic food storage bag on HIGH (100%) power for 30 seconds; knead bag to mix. Microwave at additional 10-second intervals, kneading until smooth. Cut a small hole in corner of bag; squeeze to drizzle over madeleines. Allow chocolate to cool and set before serving.

*Makes about 2½ dozen madeleines*

# Chocolate Chip Peanut Butter Swirl Cookies

**COOKIES**

½ Butter Flavor CRISCO® Stick or ½ cup Butter Flavor CRISCO® all-vegetable shortening

½ cup JIF® Creamy Peanut Butter

½ cup firmly packed light brown sugar

⅓ cup granulated sugar

1 egg

1 teaspoon vanilla

1 cup plus 1 tablespoon all-purpose flour

¾ teaspoon baking soda

½ teaspoon salt

1 cup semisweet chocolate chips, divided

**DRIZZLE**

⅓ cup miniature semisweet chocolate chips

1 teaspoon Butter Flavor CRISCO® Stick or 1 teaspoon Butter Flavor CRISCO® all-vegetable shortening

1. Heat oven to 350°F. Place sheets of foil on countertop for cooling cookies.

2. For cookies, combine ½ cup shortening and peanut butter in large bowl. Beat at medium speed of electric mixer until blended. Add brown sugar and granulated sugar gradually. Beat until well blended. Beat in egg and vanilla.

3. Combine flour, baking soda and salt. Add gradually to creamed mixture at low speed. Beat until well blended. Divide dough in half.

4. Melt ⅓ cup chocolate chips (see Melting/Drizzling Procedure). Stir into half of dough with spoon. Stir in ⅓ cup chocolate chips.

5. Stir remaining ⅓ cup chocolate chips into plain peanut butter dough.

6. Measure 1 teaspoon of each dough. Press together. Shape into 1-inch ball. Place 2 inches apart on ungreased baking sheet.

7. Bake at 350°F for about 10 minutes or until light brown and almost set. *Do not overbake.* Cool 2 minutes on baking sheet. Remove cookies to foil to cool completely.

Chip-a-licious

**8.** For drizzle, melt ⅓ cup chocolate chips and 1 teaspoon shortening (see Melting/Drizzling Procedure). Drizzle over cooled cookies.  *Makes about 3 dozen cookies*

**Melting/Drizzling Procedure:** For melting or drizzling, choose one of these easy methods. Start with chips and Butter Flavor Crisco® all-vegetable shortening (if called for), then: place in small microwave-safe measuring cup or bowl. Microwave at 50% (MEDIUM). Stir after 1 minute. Repeat until smooth. Drizzle from tip of spoon. **OR,** place in heavy resealable plastic sandwich bag. Seal. Microwave at 50% (MEDIUM). Check every minute until melted. Knead bag until smooth. Cut tiny tip off corner of bag. Squeeze out to drizzle. **OR,** place in small saucepan. Melt on range top on very low heat. Stir until smooth. Drizzle from tip of spoon.

# Chocolate Chip Shortbread

½ **cup (1 stick) butter, softened**

½ **cup sugar**

1 **teaspoon vanilla**

1 **cup all-purpose flour**

¼ **teaspoon salt**

½ **cup mini semisweet chocolate chips**

**1.** Preheat oven to 375°F.

**2.** Beat butter and sugar in large bowl with electric mixer at medium speed until light and fluffy. Beat in vanilla. Add flour and salt; beat at low speed. Stir in chips.

**3.** Divide dough in half. Press each half into *ungreased* 8-inch round cake pan.

**4.** Bake 12 minutes or until edges are golden brown. Score shortbread with sharp knife, taking care not to cut completely through shortbread. Make 8 triangles per pan.

**5.** Let pans stand on wire racks 10 minutes. Invert shortbread onto wire racks; cool completely. Break into triangles.  *Makes 16 cookies*

# Colorific Chocolate Chip Cookies

   1 cup (2 sticks) butter or margarine, softened

   ⅔ cup granulated sugar

   ½ cup firmly packed light brown sugar

   1 large egg

   1 teaspoon vanilla extract

   2 cups all-purpose flour

   ¾ teaspoon baking soda

   ¾ teaspoon salt

 1¾ cups "M&M's"® Semi-Sweet Chocolate Mini Baking Bits

   ¾ cup chopped nuts, optional

Preheat oven to 375°F. In large bowl cream butter and sugars until light and fluffy; beat in egg and vanilla. In medium bowl combine flour, baking soda and salt; blend into creamed mixture. Stir in "M&M's"® Semi-Sweet Chocolate Mini Baking Bits and nuts, if desired. Drop by heaping tablespoonfuls about 2 inches apart onto ungreased cookie sheets. Bake 9 to 12 minutes or until lightly browned. Cool 1 minute on cookie sheets; cool completely on wire racks. Store in tightly covered container.               *Makes about 3 dozen cookies*

**Hint:** For chewy cookies bake 9 to 10 minutes; for crispy cookies bake 11 to 12 minutes.

**Pan Cookie Variation:** Prepare dough as directed; spread into lightly greased 15×10×1-inch jelly-roll pan. Bake at 375°F for 18 to 22 minutes. Cool completely before cutting into 35 (2-inch) squares. For a more festive look, reserve ½ cup baking bits to sprinkle on top of dough before baking.

6 + 7 = 13   2 + 4 = 6   8 + 3 = 11

# Cinnamon Chip Gems

1 cup (2 sticks) butter or margarine, softened

2 (3-ounce) packages cream cheese, softened

2 cups all-purpose flour

½ cup sugar

⅓ cup ground toasted almonds

2 eggs

1 (14-ounce) can EAGLE BRAND® Sweetened Condensed Milk (NOT evaporated milk)

1 teaspoon vanilla extract

1⅓ cups cinnamon baking chips, divided

**1.** In large mixing bowl, beat butter and cream cheese until well blended. Stir in flour, sugar and almonds. Cover; refrigerate about 1 hour. Divide dough into 4 equal parts. Shape each part into 12 smooth balls. Place each ball in small muffin cup (1¾ inches in diameter); press evenly on bottom and up side of each cup.

**2.** Preheat oven to 375°F. In small mixing bowl, beat eggs. Add Eagle Brand and vanilla; mix well. Place 7 cinnamon baking chips in bottom of each muffin cup; generously fill three-fourths full with Eagle Brand mixture.

**3.** Bake 18 to 20 minutes or until tops are puffed and just beginning to turn golden brown. Cool 3 minutes. Sprinkle about 15 chips on top of filling. Cool completely in pan on wire rack. Remove from pan using small metal spatula or sharp knife. Cool completely. Store tightly covered at room temperature. *Makes 4 dozen cookies*

**Tip:** For a pretty presentation, line the muffin pan with colorful paper baking cups before pressing the dough into the muffin cups.

6 + 7 = 13   2 + 4 = 6   8 + 3 = 11

# Mini Chip Snowball Cookies

1½ cups (3 sticks) butter or margarine, softened

¾ cup powdered sugar

1 tablespoon vanilla extract

½ teaspoon salt

3 cups all-purpose flour

2 cups (12-ounce package) NESTLÉ® TOLL HOUSE® Semi-Sweet Chocolate Mini Morsels

½ cup finely chopped nuts

Powdered sugar

**PREHEAT** oven to 375°F.

**BEAT** butter, sugar, vanilla extract and salt in large mixer bowl until creamy. Gradually beat in flour; stir in morsels and nuts. Shape level tablespoons of dough into 1¼-inch balls. Place on ungreased baking sheets.

**BAKE** for 10 to 12 minutes or until cookies are set and lightly browned. Remove from oven. Sift powdered sugar over hot cookies on baking sheets. Cool on baking sheets for 10 minutes; remove to wire racks to cool completely. Sprinkle with additional powdered sugar, if desired. Store in airtight containers.

*Makes about 5 dozen cookies*

92

Chip-a-licious

6 + 7 = 13    2 + 4 = 6    8 + 3 = 11

# Oatmeal Coconut Chocolate Chip Cookies

**COOKIES**

1 Butter Flavor CRISCO® Stick or 1 cup Butter Flavor CRISCO® all-vegetable shortening plus additional for greasing

1 cup granulated sugar

½ cup firmly packed light brown sugar

2 eggs

2 teaspoons vanilla

2 cups all-purpose flour

1 teaspoon salt

1 teaspoon baking soda

⅔ cup quick oats, uncooked

½ cup flake coconut

1 cup semisweet chocolate chips

**CHOCOLATE COATING**

1 cup semisweet chocolate chips

2 teaspoons Butter Flavor CRISCO® Stick or 2 teaspoons Butter Flavor CRISCO® all-vegetable shortening

1. Heat oven to 375°F. Grease baking sheet with shortening. Place sheets of foil on countertop for cooling cookies.

2. For cookies, combine 1 cup shortening, granulated sugar, brown sugar, eggs and vanilla in large bowl. Beat at medium speed of electric mixer until well blended.

3. Combine flour, salt and baking soda. Add gradually to creamed mixture at low speed. Beat until well blended. Stir in oats, coconut and 1 cup chocolate chips with spoon. Drop by teaspoonfuls 2 inches apart onto prepared baking sheet.

4. Bake at 375°F for 10 to 12 minutes or until light brown. *Do not overbake.* Cool 2 minutes on baking sheet. Remove cookies to foil to cool completely.

5. For chocolate coating, melt 1 cup chocolate chips and 2 teaspoons shortening (see Melting/Drizzling Procedure).

**6.** Spread thin coating of melted chocolate on back of each cookie. Place upside down on waxed paper to allow coating to harden.

*Makes about 6 dozen cookies*

**Melting/Drizzling Procedure:** For melting or drizzling, choose one of these easy methods. Start with chips and Butter Flavor Crisco® all-vegetable shortening (if called for), then: place in small microwave-safe measuring cup or bowl. Microwave at 50% (MEDIUM). Stir after 1 minute. Repeat until smooth. Drizzle from tip of spoon. Or, place chips and shortening in heavy resealable plastic sandwich bag. Seal. Microwave at 50% (MEDIUM). Check every minute until melted. Knead bag until smooth. Cut tiny tip off corner of bag. Squeeze out to drizzle. Or, place chips and shortening in small saucepan. Melt on range top on very low heat. Stir until smooth. Drizzle from tip of spoon.

# Peanut Butter Chocolate Chippers

> **1 cup creamy or chunky peanut butter**
> **1 cup packed light brown sugar**
> **1 large egg**
> **¾ cup milk chocolate chips**
> **Granulated sugar**

**1.** Preheat oven to 350°F.

**2.** Combine peanut butter, brown sugar and egg in medium bowl; mix until well blended. Add chips; mix well.

**3.** Roll heaping tablespoonfuls of dough into 1½-inch balls. Place balls 2 inches apart on ungreased cookie sheets.

**4.** Dip table fork into granulated sugar; press criss-cross fashion onto each ball, flattening to ½-inch thickness.

**5.** Bake 12 minutes or until set. Let cookies stand on cookie sheets 2 minutes. Remove cookies with spatula to wire racks; cool completely.

*Makes about 2 dozen cookies*

**Note:** This simple recipe is unusual because it doesn't contain any flour—but it still makes great cookies!

95

*Chip-a-licious*

# Dreamy Chocolate Chip Cookies

1¼ cups firmly packed brown sugar

¾ Butter Flavor CRISCO® Stick or ¾ cup Butter Flavor CRISCO® all-vegetable shortening

3 eggs, lightly beaten

2 teaspoons vanilla

1 (4-ounce) package German sweet chocolate, melted, cooled

3 cups all-purpose flour

1 teaspoon baking soda

½ teaspoon salt

1 (11½-ounce) package milk chocolate chips

1 (10-ounce) package premium semisweet chocolate pieces

1 cup coarsely chopped macadamia nuts

**1.** Heat oven to 375°F. Place sheets of foil on countertop for cooling cookies.

**2.** Combine brown sugar, ¾ cup shortening, eggs and vanilla in large bowl. Beat at low speed of electric mixer until blended. Increase speed to high. Beat 2 minutes. Add melted chocolate. Mix until well blended.

**3.** Combine flour, baking soda and salt. Add gradually to shortening mixture at low speed.

**4.** Stir in chocolate chips, chocolate pieces and nuts with spoon. Drop by rounded tablespoonfuls 3 inches apart onto ungreased baking sheets.

**5.** Bake at 375°F for 9 to 11 minutes or until set. *Do not overbake.* Cool 2 minutes on baking sheet. Remove cookies to foil to cool completely.                    *Makes about 3 dozen cookies*

6 + 7 = 13    2 + 4 = 6    8 + 3 = 11

# Sour Cream Chocolate Chip Cookies

1 Butter Flavor CRISCO® Stick or 1 cup Butter Flavor CRISCO® all-vegetable shortening plus additional for greasing

1 cup firmly packed light brown sugar

½ cup granulated sugar

1 egg

½ cup dairy sour cream

¼ cup warm honey

2 teaspoons vanilla

2½ cups all-purpose flour

1½ teaspoons baking powder

½ teaspoon salt

2 cups semisweet or milk chocolate chips

1 cup coarsely chopped walnuts

**1.** Heat oven to 375°F. Grease cookie sheet. Place sheets of foil on countertop for cooling cookies.

**2.** Combine 1 cup shortening, brown sugar and granulated sugar in large bowl. Beat at medium speed of electric mixer until well blended. Beat in egg, sour cream, honey and vanilla. Beat until just blended.

**3.** Combine flour, baking powder and salt. Mix into creamed mixture at low speed until just blended. Stir in chocolate chips and nuts.

**4.** Drop slightly rounded measuring tablespoonfuls of dough 2 inches apart onto prepared sheet.

**5.** Bake at 375°F 10 to 12 minutes or until set. *Do not overbake.* Cool 2 minutes on baking sheet. Remove to foil to cool completely.                    *Makes about 5 dozen cookies*

6 + 7 = 13   2 + 4 = 6   8 + 3 = 11

# Pineapple and White Chip Drops

1 cup (2 sticks) butter or margarine, softened

1 cup sugar

2 eggs

½ teaspoon vanilla extract

1 can (8 ounces) crushed pineapple, with juice

3½ cups all-purpose flour

1 teaspoon baking soda

¾ teaspoon ground cinnamon

½ teaspoon salt

¼ teaspoon ground nutmeg

1 cup chopped pecans

1⅔ cups (10-ounce package) HERSHEY'S Premier White Chips

**1.** Heat oven to 350°F. Lightly grease cookie sheet.

**2.** Beat butter and sugar in large bowl until well blended. Add eggs and vanilla; blend well. Blend in pineapple and juice. Stir together flour, baking soda, cinnamon, salt and nutmeg; gradually add to butter mixture, beating until well blended. Stir in pecans and white chips. Drop by tablespoons onto prepared cookie sheet.

**3.** Bake 10 to 12 minutes or until lightly browned around edges. Remove from cookie sheet to wire rack. Cool completely.

*Makes about 5 dozen cookies*

6 + 7 = 13    2 + 4 = 6    8 + 3 = 11

# Bar-o-metrics

## Crispy Rice Squares

**3 tablespoons Dried Plum Purée (recipe follows) or prepared dried plum butter**

**1 tablespoon butter or margarine**

**1 package (10 ounces) marshmallows**

**6 cups crisp rice cereal**

**Colored nonpareils**

Coat 13×9-inch baking pan with vegetable cooking spray. Heat dried plum purée and butter in Dutch oven or large saucepan over low heat, stirring until butter is melted. Add marshmallows; stir until completely melted. Remove from heat. Stir in cereal until well coated. Spray back of wooden spoon with vegetable cooking spray and pat mixture evenly into prepared pan. Sprinkle with nonpareils. Cool until set. Cut into squares. *Makes 24 squares*

**Dried Plum Purée:** Combine 1⅓ cups (8 ounces) pitted dried plums and 6 tablespoons hot water in container of food processor or blender. Pulse on and off until dried plums are finely chopped and smooth. Store leftovers in a covered container in the refrigerator for up to two months. Makes 1 cup.

Favorite recipe from **California Dried Plum Board**

# Razz-Ma-Tazz Bars

½ cup (1 stick) butter or margarine

2 cups (12-ounce package) NESTLÉ® TOLL HOUSE® Premier White Morsels, *divided*

2 large eggs

½ cup granulated sugar

1 cup all-purpose flour

½ teaspoon salt

½ teaspoon almond extract

½ cup seedless raspberry jam

¼ cup toasted sliced almonds

**PREHEAT** oven to 325°F. Grease and sugar 9-inch-square baking pan.

**MELT** butter in medium, microwave-safe bowl on HIGH (100%) power for 1 minute; stir. Add *1 cup* morsels; let stand. Do not stir.

**BEAT** eggs in large mixer bowl until foamy. Add sugar; beat until light lemon colored, about 5 minutes. Stir in morsel-butter mixture. Add flour, salt and almond extract; mix at low speed until combined. Spread ⅔ of batter into prepared pan.

**BAKE** for 15 to 17 minutes or until light golden brown around edges. Remove from oven to wire rack.

**HEAT** jam in small, microwave-safe bowl on HIGH (100%) power for 30 seconds; stir. Spread jam over warm crust. Stir *remaining* morsels into *remaining* batter. Drop spoonfuls of batter over jam. Sprinkle with almonds.

**BAKE** for 25 to 30 minutes or until edges are browned. Cool completely in pan on wire rack. Cut into bars. *Makes 16 bars*

# "Everything but the Kitchen Sink" Bar Cookies

**1 package (18 ounces) refrigerated chocolate chip cookie dough**
**1 jar (7 ounces) marshmallow creme**
**½ cup creamy peanut butter**
**1½ cups toasted corn cereal**
**½ cup miniature candy-coated chocolate pieces**

**1.** Preheat oven to 350°F. Grease 13×9-inch baking pan. Remove dough from wrapper according to package directions.

**2.** Press dough into prepared baking pan. Bake 13 minutes.

**3.** Remove baking pan from oven. Drop teaspoonfuls of marshmallow creme and peanut butter over hot cookie base.

**4.** Bake 1 minute. Carefully spread marshmallow creme and peanut butter over cookie base.

**5.** Sprinkle cereal and chocolate pieces over melted marshmallow and peanut butter mixture.

**6.** Bake 7 minutes. Cool completely on wire rack. Cut into 2-inch bars.     *Makes 3 dozen bars*

# Chocolate Chip Cookie Bars

1¼ cups firmly packed light brown sugar

¾ Butter Flavor CRISCO® Stick or ¾ cup Butter Flavor CRISCO® all-vegetable shortening plus additional for greasing

2 tablespoons milk

1 tablespoon vanilla

2 eggs

1¾ cups all-purpose flour

1 teaspoon salt

¾ teaspoon baking soda

1 cup (6 ounces) semisweet chocolate chips

1 cup coarsely chopped pecans* (optional)

*If pecans are omitted, add an additional ½ cup semisweet chocolate chips.*

**1.** Heat oven to 350°F. Grease 13×9-inch baking pan. Place wire rack on countertop for cooling bars.

**2.** Combine brown sugar, shortening, milk and vanilla in large bowl. Beat at medium speed of electric mixer until well blended. Add eggs; beat well.

**3.** Combine flour, salt and baking soda. Add to shortening mixture; beat at low speed just until blended. Stir in chocolate chips and nuts, if desired.

**4.** Press dough evenly onto bottom of prepared pan.

**5.** Bake at 350°F for 20 to 25 minutes or until lightly browned and firm in the center. *Do not overbake.* Cool completely on cooling rack. Cut into 2×1½-inch bars.

*Makes about 3 dozen bars*

# Peanut Butter and Jelly Crispies

½ Butter Flavor CRISCO® Stick or ½ cup Butter Flavor CRISCO® all-vegetable shortening
plus additional for greasing

½ cup JIF® Crunchy Peanut Butter

½ cup granulated sugar

½ cup firmly packed light brown sugar

1 egg

1¼ cups all-purpose flour

½ teaspoon baking powder

½ teaspoon baking soda

¼ teaspoon salt

2 cups crisp rice cereal

Honey roasted peanuts, finely chopped (optional)

SMUCKER'S® Jelly, any flavor

**1.** Heat oven to 375°F. Grease 13×9×2-inch pan with shortening. Place wire rack on countertop for cooling bars.

**2.** Combine ½ cup shortening, peanut butter, granulated sugar and brown sugar in large bowl. Beat at medium speed of electric mixer until well blended. Beat in egg.

**3.** Combine flour, baking powder, baking soda and salt. Add gradually to creamed mixture at low speed. Beat until well blended. Add cereal. Mix just until blended. Press into greased pan. Sprinkle with nuts, if desired.

**4.** Score dough into bars about 2¼×2 inches. Press thumb in center of each. Fill indentation with ¼ to ½ teaspoon jelly.

**5.** Bake at 375°F for 12 to 15 minutes or until golden brown. *Do not overbake.* Remove pan to wire rack. Cool 2 to 3 minutes. Cut into bars. Cool completely.          *Makes about 2 dozen bars*

# Rocky Road Bars

2 cups (12-ounce package) NESTLÉ® TOLL HOUSE® Semi-Sweet Chocolate Morsels, *divided*

1½ cups all-purpose flour

1½ teaspoons baking powder

1 cup granulated sugar

6 tablespoons (¾ stick) butter or margarine, softened

1½ teaspoons vanilla extract

2 large eggs

2 cups miniature marshmallows

1½ cups coarsely chopped walnuts

**PREHEAT** oven to 375°F. Grease 13×9-inch baking pan.

**MICROWAVE** *1 cup* morsels in medium, uncovered, microwave-safe bowl on HIGH (100%) power for 1 minute. STIR. Morsels may retain some of their original shape. If necessary, microwave at additional 10- to 15-second intervals, stirring just until morsels are melted. Cool to room temperature. Combine flour and baking powder in small bowl.

**BEAT** sugar, butter and vanilla in large mixer bowl until crumbly. Beat in eggs. Add melted chocolate; beat until smooth. Gradually beat in flour mixture. Spread batter into prepared baking pan.

**BAKE** for 16 to 20 minutes or until wooden pick inserted in center comes out slightly sticky.

**REMOVE** from oven; sprinkle immediately with marshmallows, nuts and *remaining* morsels. Return to oven for 2 minutes or just until marshmallows begin to melt. Cool in pan on wire rack for 20 to 30 minutes. Cut into bars with wet knife. Serve warm. *Makes 2½ dozen bars*

# Cookie Pizza

**1 (18-ounce) package refrigerated sugar cookie dough**

**2 cups (12 ounces) semi-sweet chocolate chips**

**1 (14-ounce) can EAGLE BRAND® Sweetened Condensed Milk (NOT evaporated milk)**

**2 cups candy-coated milk chocolate candies**

**2 cups miniature marshmallows**

**½ cup peanuts**

**1.** Preheat oven 375°F. Press cookie dough into 2 ungreased 12-inch pizza pans. Bake 10 minutes or until golden. Remove from oven.

**2.** In medium-sized saucepan, melt chips with Eagle Brand. Spread over crusts. Sprinkle with milk chocolate candies, marshmallows and peanuts.

**3.** Bake 4 minutes or until marshmallows are lightly toasted. Cool. Cut into wedges.

*Makes 2 pizzas (24 servings)*

**Prep Time:** 15 minutes
**Bake Time:** 14 minutes

Bar-o-metrics

# Blueberry Cheesecake Bars

   1 package DUNCAN HINES® Bakery-Style Blueberry Streusel Muffin Mix
   ¼ cup cold butter or margarine
   ⅓ cup finely chopped pecans
   1 package (8 ounces) cream cheese, softened
   ½ cup sugar
   1 egg
   3 tablespoons lemon juice
   1 teaspoon grated lemon peel

**1.** Preheat oven to 350°F. Grease 9-inch square baking pan.

**2.** Rinse blueberries from Mix with cold water and drain; set aside.

**3.** Place muffin mix in medium bowl; cut in butter with pastry blender or two knives. Stir in pecans. Press into bottom of prepared pan. Bake at 350°F for 15 minutes or until set.

**4.** Combine cream cheese and sugar in medium bowl. Beat until smooth. Add egg, lemon juice and lemon peel. Beat well. Spread over baked crust. Sprinkle with blueberries. Sprinkle topping packet from Mix over blueberries. Return to oven. Bake at 350°F for 35 to 40 minutes or until filling is set. Cool completely. Refrigerate until ready to serve. Cut into bars.

*Makes about 16 bars*

# Peanut Bars

**Cookie Base**

½ CRISCO® Stick or ½ cup CRISCO® all-vegetable shortening plus additional for greasing

1¼ cups firmly packed light brown sugar

¾ cup JIF® Creamy Peanut Butter

3 tablespoons milk

1½ teaspoons vanilla

½ teaspoon almond extract

1 egg

1¾ cups all-purpose flour

¾ teaspoon baking soda

¾ teaspoon salt

2 cups (12 ounce) package peanut butter chips, divided

**Drizzle**

½ cup confectioners' sugar

¼ cup JIF® Creamy Peanut Butter

2 to 4 tablespoons milk

**1.** Heat oven to 350°F. Grease 13×9 baking pan.

**2.** For cookie base, combine shortening, brown sugar, peanut butter, milk, vanilla and almond extract in large bowl. Beat at medium speed of electric mixer until well blended. Add egg. Beat just until blended.

**3.** Combine flour, baking soda and salt. Add to creamed mixture at low speed. Mix just until blended. Stir in 1 cup peanut butter chips. Press mixture into prepared pan.

**4.** Bake at 350°F for 20 minutes. Remove from oven and sprinkle with remaining 1 cup peanut butter chips. Let stand 5 minutes or until chips melt. Spread evenly over surface. (Or, return to oven briefly to melt chips and spread evenly over surface.) Let sit until pan cools and melted chips harden.

**5.** For drizzle, combine confectioners' sugar, peanut butter and milk in small bowl. Beat well. Drizzle over cooled bars.

**6.** Cut into approximately 2¼×1-inch bars.

*Makes about 4½ dozen bars*

# Emily's Dream Bars

½ Butter Flavor CRISCO® Stick or ½ cup Butter Flavor CRISCO® all-vegetable shortening plus additional for greasing

1 cup JIF® Crunchy Peanut Butter

½ cup firmly packed brown sugar

½ cup light corn syrup

1 egg

1 teaspoon vanilla

1 cup all-purpose flour

½ teaspoon baking powder

¼ cup milk

2 cups 100% natural oats, honey and raisins cereal

1 package (12 ounces) miniature semisweet chocolate chips (2 cups), divided

1 cup almond brickle chips

1 cup milk chocolate covered peanuts

1 package (2 ounces) nut topping (⅓ cup)

**1.** Heat oven to 350°F. Grease 13×9×2-inch pan with shortening. Place wire rack on countertop for cooling bars.

**2.** Combine ½ cup shortening, peanut butter, brown sugar and corn syrup in large bowl. Beat at medium speed of electric mixer until creamy. Add egg and vanilla. Beat well.

**3.** Combine flour and baking powder. Add alternately with milk to creamed mixture at medium speed. Stir in cereal, 1 cup chocolate chips, almond brickle chips and chocolate covered nuts with spoon. Spread in prepared pan.

**4.** Bake at 350°F for 20 to 26 minutes or until golden brown and toothpick inserted in center comes out clean. *Do not overbake.* Sprinkle remaining 1 cup chocolate chips over top immediately after removing from oven. Remove pan to wire rack. Let stand about 3 minutes or until chips become shiny and soft. Spread over top. Sprinkle with nut topping. Cool completely. Cut into 2×1-inch bars. *Makes 4½ dozen bars*

# Chocolate Cream Cheese Sugar Cookie Bars

    1 package (22.3 ounces) golden sugar cookie mix
    3 eggs, divided
    ⅓ cup plus 6 tablespoons butter or margarine, softened and divided
    1 teaspoon water
    1 package (8 ounces) cream cheese, softened
    1 package (3 ounces) cream cheese, softened
    ¾ cup granulated sugar
    ⅓ cup HERSHEY'S Cocoa
  1½ teaspoons vanilla extract
      Powdered sugar

**1.** Heat oven to 350°F.

**2.** Empty cookie mix into large bowl. Break up any lumps. Add 2 eggs, ⅓ cup butter and water; stir with spoon or fork until well blended. Spread into ungreased 13×9×2-inch baking pan.

**3.** Beat cream cheese and remaining 6 tablespoons butter in medium bowl on medium speed of mixer until fluffy. Stir together granulated sugar and cocoa; gradually add to cream cheese mixture, beating until smooth and well blended. Add remaining egg and vanilla; beat well. Spread cream cheese mixture evenly over cookie batter.

**4.** Bake 35 to 40 minutes or until no imprint remains when touched lightly in center. Cool completely in pan on wire rack. Sprinkle powdered sugar over top. Cut into bars. Cover; store leftover bars in refrigerator. *Makes about 24 to 30 bars*

# Irish Flag Cookies

1½ cups all-purpose flour

1 teaspoon baking powder

½ teaspoon salt

¾ cup granulated sugar

¾ cup light brown sugar

½ cup (1 stick) butter, softened

2 eggs

2 teaspoons vanilla

1 package (10 ounces) semisweet chocolate chips

Prepared white frosting

Green and orange food coloring

**1.** Preheat oven to 350°F. Grease 13×9-inch baking pan. Combine flour, baking powder and salt in small bowl; set aside.

**2.** Beat granulated sugar, brown sugar and butter in large bowl with electric mixer at medium speed until light and fluffy. Beat in eggs and vanilla. Add flour mixture. Beat at low speed until well blended. Stir in chocolate chips and macadamia nuts. Spread batter evenly in prepared pan. Bake 25 to 30 minutes or until golden brown. Remove pan to wire rack; cool completely. Cut into 3¼×1½-inch bars.

**3.** Divide frosting among 3 small bowls. Tint 1 with orange food coloring; 1 with green. Leave remaining frosting white. Frost individual cookies as shown in photo.      *Makes 2 dozen cookies*

# Butterscotch Blondies

¾ **cup (1½ sticks) butter or margarine, softened**
¾ **cup packed light brown sugar**
½ **cup granulated sugar**
2 **eggs**
2 **cups all-purpose flour**
1 **teaspoon baking soda**
½ **teaspoon salt**
1⅔ **cups (10-ounce package) HERSHEY'S Butterscotch Chips**
1 **cup chopped nuts (optional)**

**1.** Heat oven to 350°F. Grease 13×9×2-inch baking pan.

**2.** Beat butter, brown sugar and granulated sugar in large bowl until creamy. Add eggs; beat well. Stir together flour, baking soda and salt; gradually add to butter mixture, blending well. Stir in butterscotch chips and nuts, if desired. Spread into prepared pan.

**3.** Bake 30 to 35 minutes or until top is golden brown and center is set. Cool completely in pan on wire rack. Cut into bars.
*Makes about 36 bars*

# Mystical Layered Bars

⅓ cup butter

1 cup graham cracker crumbs

½ cup uncooked old-fashioned or quick oats

1 can (14 ounces) sweetened condensed milk

1 cup flaked coconut

¾ cup semisweet chocolate chips

¾ cup raisins

1 cup coarsely chopped pecans

Preheat oven to 350°F. Melt butter in 13×9-inch baking pan. Remove from oven.

Sprinkle graham cracker crumbs and oats evenly over butter; press with fork. Drizzle condensed milk over oats. Layer coconut, chocolate chips, raisins and pecans over milk.

Bake 25 to 30 minutes or until lightly browned. Cool in pan on wire rack 5 minutes; cut into 2×1½-inch bars. Cool completely in pan on wire rack. Store tightly covered at room temperature or freeze up to 3 months.                               *Makes 3 dozen bars*

# Chocolate Peanutty Crumble Bars

½ cup butter or margarine

1 cup all-purpose flour

¾ cup instant oats, uncooked

⅓ cup firmly packed brown sugar

½ teaspoon baking soda

½ teaspoon vanilla extract

4 SNICKERS® Bars (2.07 ounces each), cut into 8 slices each

Preheat oven to 350°F. Grease bottom of an 8-inch square pan. Melt butter in large saucepan. Remove from heat and stir in flour, oats, brown sugar, baking soda and vanilla. Blend until crumbly. Press ⅔ of the mixture into prepared pan. Arrange SNICKERS® Bar slices in pan, about ½ inch from the edge of pan. Finely crumble the remaining mixture over the sliced SNICKERS® Bars. Bake for 25 minutes or until edges are golden brown. Cool in pan on cooling rack. Cut into bars or squares to serve.

*Makes 24 bars*

## Candy Bar Bars

¾ cup (1½ sticks) butter or margarine, softened

¼ cup peanut butter

1 cup firmly packed light brown sugar

1 teaspoon baking soda

2 cups quick-cooking oats

1½ cups all-purpose flour

1 egg

1 (14-ounce) can EAGLE BRAND® Sweetened Condensed Milk (NOT evaporated milk)

4 cups chopped candy bars (such as chocolate-coated caramel-topped nougat bars with peanuts, chocolate-covered crisp wafers, chocolate-covered caramel-topped cookie bars, or chocolate-covered peanut butter cups)

**1.** Preheat oven to 350°F. In large mixing bowl, combine butter and peanut butter. Add brown sugar and baking soda; beat well. Stir in oats and flour. Reserve 1¾ cups crumb mixture.

**2.** Stir egg into remaining crumb mixture; press firmly on bottom of ungreased 15×10×1-inch baking pan. Bake 15 minutes.

**3.** Pour Eagle Brand evenly over baked crust. Stir together reserved crumb mixture and candy bar pieces; sprinkle evenly over top. Bake 25 minutes or until golden. Cool. Cut into bars. Store covered at room temperature.

*Makes 4 dozen bars*

**Prep Time:** 20 minutes
**Bake Time:** 40 minutes

# Snack Time

## S'Mores on a Stick

1 (14-ounce) can EAGLE BRAND® Sweetened Condensed Milk (NOT evaporated milk), divided

1½ cups milk chocolate mini chips, divided

1 cup miniature marshmallows

11 whole graham crackers, halved crosswise

Toppings: chopped peanuts, mini candy-coated chocolate pieces, sprinkles

**1.** Microwave half of Eagle Brand in microwave-safe bowl at HIGH (100% power) 1½ minutes. Stir in 1 cup chips until smooth; stir in marshmallows.

**2.** Spread evenly by heaping tablespoonfuls onto 11 graham cracker halves. Top with remaining graham cracker halves; place on waxed paper.

**3.** Microwave remaining Eagle Brand at HIGH (100% power) 1½ minutes; stir in remaining ½ cup chips, stirring until smooth. Drizzle mixture over cookies and sprinkle with desired toppings.

**4.** Let stand for 2 hours; insert a wooden craft stick into center of each cookie.

*Makes 11 servings*

**Prep Time:** 10 minutes
**Cook Time:** 3 minutes

# Super Spread Sandwich Stars

**1 Red or Golden Delicious apple, peeled, cored and coarsely chopped**

**1 cup roasted peanuts**

**⅓ cup honey**

**1 tablespoon lemon juice**

**1 teaspoon ground cinnamon**

**Sliced sandwich bread**

For Super Spread, place chopped apple, peanuts, honey, lemon juice and cinnamon in food processor or blender. Pulse food processor several times until ingredients start to blend, occasionally scraping down the sides with rubber spatula. Process 1 to 2 minutes until mixture is smooth and spreadable.

For Sandwich Stars, use butter knife to spread about 1 tablespoon Super Spread on 2 slices of bread. Stack them together, spread side up. Top with third slice bread. Place cookie cutter on top of sandwich; press down firmly and evenly. Leaving cookie cutter in place, remove excess trimmings with your fingers or a butter knife. Remove cookie cutter.

*Makes 1¼ cups spread (enough for about 10 sandwiches)*

Favorite recipe from **Texas Peanut Producers Board**

# Soft Pretzels

**1 package (16 ounces) hot roll mix plus ingredients to prepare mix**

**1 egg white**

**2 teaspoons water**

**2 tablespoons *each* assorted coatings: coarse salt, sesame seeds, poppy seeds, dried oregano leaves**

**1.** Prepare hot roll mix according to package directions.

**2.** Preheat oven to 375°F. Spray baking sheets with nonstick cooking spray; set aside.

**3.** Divide dough equally into 16 pieces; roll each piece with hands to form rope, 7 to 10 inches long. Place on prepared cookie sheets; form into desired shape (hearts, wreaths, pretzels, snails, loops, etc.).

**4.** Beat egg white and water in small bowl until foamy. Brush onto dough shapes; sprinkle each shape with 1½ teaspoons of one coating.

**5.** Bake until golden brown, about 15 minutes. Serve warm or at room temperature.

*Makes 8 servings*

**Fruit Twists:** Omit coatings. Prepare dough and roll into ropes as directed. Place ropes on lightly floured surface. Roll out, or pat, each rope into rectangle, ¼ inch thick; brush each rectangle with about 1 teaspoon spreadable fruit or preserves. Fold each rectangle lengthwise in half; twist into desired shape. Bake as directed.

**Cheese Twists:** Omit coatings. Prepare dough and roll into ropes as directed. Place ropes on lightly floured surface. Roll out, or pat, each rope into rectangle, ¼ inch thick. Sprinkle each rectangle with about 1 tablespoon shredded Cheddar or other flavor cheese. Fold each rectangle lengthwise in half; twist into desired shape. Bake as directed.

 duck  bird  pig

# Take-Along Snack Mix

1 tablespoon butter or margarine

2 tablespoons honey

1 cup toasted oat cereal, any flavor

½ cup coarsely broken pecans

½ cup thin pretzel sticks, broken in half

½ cup raisins

1 cup "M&M's"® Chocolate Mini Baking Bits

In large heavy skillet over low heat, melt butter; add honey and stir until blended. Add cereal, nuts, pretzels and raisins, stirring until all pieces are evenly coated. Continue cooking over low heat about 10 minutes, stirring frequently. Remove from heat; immediately spread on waxed paper until cool. Add "M&M's"® Chocolate Mini Baking Bits. Store in tightly covered container.

*Makes about 3½ cups*

# Taco Popcorn Olé

9 cups air-popped popcorn

Butter-flavored cooking spray

1 teaspoon chili powder

½ teaspoon *each* salt and garlic powder

⅛ teaspoon ground red pepper (optional)

Preheat oven to 350°F. Line 15×10-inch jelly-roll pan with foil. Place popcorn in single layer in prepared pan. Coat lightly with cooking spray. Combine chili powder, salt, garlic powder and red pepper, if desired, in small bowl; sprinkle over popcorn. Mix lightly to coat evenly. Bake 5 minutes or until hot, stirring gently after 3 minutes. Spread mixture in single layer on large sheet of foil to cool.

*Makes 6 (1½-cup) servings*

**Tip:** Store popcorn mixture in tightly covered container at room temperature up to 4 days.

 duck  bird  pig

# Cinnamon Apple Chips

**2 cups unsweetened apple juice**
**1 cinnamon stick**
**2 Washington Red Delicious apples**

**1.** In large skillet or saucepan, combine apple juice and cinnamon stick; bring to a low boil while preparing apples.

**2.** With paring knife, slice off ½ inch from tops and bottoms of apples and discard (or eat). Stand apples on either cut end; cut crosswise into ⅛-inch-thick slices, rotating apple as necessary to cut even slices.

**3.** Drop slices into boiling juice; cook 4 to 5 minutes or until slices appear translucent and lightly golden. Meanwhile, preheat oven to 250°F.

**4.** With slotted spatula, remove apple slices from juice and pat dry. Arrange slices on wire racks, being sure none overlap. Place racks on middle shelf in oven; bake 30 to 40 minutes until slices are lightly browned and almost dry to touch. Let chips cool on racks completely before storing in airtight container. *Makes about 40 chips*

**Tip:** There is no need to core apples because boiling in juice for several minutes softens core and removes seeds.

Favorite recipe from **Washington Apple Commission**

 duck  bird  pig

# Dipped, Drizzled & Decorated Pretzels

**1 bag chocolate or flavored chips (choose semisweet, bittersweet, milk chocolate, green mint, white chocolate, butterscotch, peanut butter or a combination)**

**1 bag pretzel rods**

**Assorted toppings: jimmies, sprinkles, chopped nuts, coconut, toasted coconut, cookie crumbs, colored sugars (optional)**

**Microwave Directions**

**1.** Place chips in microwavable bowl. (Be sure bowl and utensils are completely dry.) Cover with plastic wrap and turn back one corner to vent. Microwave at HIGH for 1 minute; stir. Return to microwave and continue cooking in 30-second intervals until chips are completely melted. Check and stir frequently.

**2.** Dip one half of each pretzel rod into melted chocolate and decorate, if desired. Roll coated end of several pretzels in toppings. Drizzle others with contrasting color/flavor melted chips. (Drizzle melted chocolate out of spoon while rotating pretzel, to get even coverage.)

**3.** Place decorated pretzels on cooling rack; set over baking sheet lined with waxed-paper. Let coating harden completely. Do not refrigerate. *Makes about 2 dozen pretzels*

# Sweet Treat Tortillas

**4 (7- to 8-inch) flour tortillas**

**4 ounces Neufchatel cheese, softened**

**¼ cup strawberry or other flavor spreadable fruit or preserves**

**1 medium banana, peeled and chopped**

**1.** Spread each tortilla with 1 ounce Neufchatel cheese and 1 tablespoon spreadable fruit; top with ¼ of the banana.

**2.** Roll up tortillas; cut crosswise into thirds.

*Makes 6 servings*

**More Sweet Treats:** Substitute your favorite chopped fruit for banana.

**Cinnamon-Spice Treats:** Omit spreadable fruit and banana. Mix small amounts of sugar, ground cinnamon and nutmeg into Neufchatel cheese; spread evenly onto tortillas. Sprinkle lightly with desired amount of chopped pecans or walnuts. Top with chopped fruit, if desired; roll up. Cut crosswise into thirds.

# Super nachos

**12 large baked low-fat tortilla chips (about 1½ ounces)**
**½ cup (2 ounces) shredded reduced-fat Cheddar cheese**
**¼ cup fat-free refried beans**
**2 tablespoons chunky salsa**

**1.** Arrange chips in single layer on large microwavable plate. Sprinkle cheese evenly over chips.

**2.** Spoon teaspoonfuls of beans over chips; top with ½ teaspoonfuls of salsa.

**3.** Microwave at MEDIUM (50%) 1½ minutes; rotate dish. Microwave 1 to 1½ minutes or until cheese is melted.

*Makes 2 servings*

**Conventional Directions:** Substitute foil-covered baking sheet for microwavable plate. Assemble nachos as directed on prepared baking sheet. Bake at 350°F for 10 to 12 minutes or until cheese is melted.

**Cook's Tip:** For a single serving of nachos, arrange 6 large tortilla chips on microwavable plate; top with ¼ cup cheese, 2 tablespoons refried beans and 1 tablespoon salsa. Microwave at MEDIUM (50%) 1 minute; rotate dish. Continue to microwave 30 seconds to 1 minute or until cheese is melted.

# Purple Cow Jumped Over the Moon

**3 cups vanilla nonfat frozen yogurt**

**1 cup reduced-fat (2%) milk**

**½ cup thawed frozen grape juice concentrate (undiluted)**

**1½ teaspoons lemon juice**

Place yogurt, milk, grape juice concentrate and lemon juice in food processor or blender container; process until smooth. Serve immediately. *Makes 8 (½-cup) servings*

**Razzmatazz Shake:** Place 1 quart vanilla nonfat frozen yogurt, 1 cup vanilla nonfat yogurt and ¼ cup chocolate nonfat syrup in food processor or blender container; process until smooth. Pour ½ of mixture evenly into 12 glasses; top with ½ of (12-ounce) can root beer. Fill glasses equally with remaining yogurt mixture; top with remaining root beer. Makes 12 (⅔-cup) servings.

**Sunshine Shake:** Place 1 quart vanilla nonfat frozen yogurt, 1⅓ cups orange juice, 1 cup fresh or thawed frozen raspberries and 1 teaspoon sugar in food processor or blender container; process until smooth. Pour into 10 glasses; sprinkle with ground nutmeg. Makes 10 (½-cup) servings.

## Caramel Popcorn Balls

16 cups plain popped popcorn (do not use buttered popcorn)
1 package (14 ounces) caramels, unwrapped
¼ cup butter
   Pinch of salt
1⅔ cups shredded sweetened coconut
1 package (12 ounces) semisweet chocolate chips
10 to 12 lollipop sticks
   Halloween sprinkles and decorations (optional)

1. Place popcorn in large bowl.

2. In medium saucepan over low heat, place caramels and butter. Cook and stir until caramels and butter are melted and smooth, about 5 minutes. Stir in salt and coconut. Remove caramel mixture from heat; pour over popcorn. With large wooden spoon, mix until popcorn is evenly coated. Let cool slightly.

3. Place chocolate chips in microwavable bowl. Microwave at HIGH 1 minute; stir. Microwave at HIGH for additional 30-second intervals until chips are completely melted, stirring after each 30-second interval. Stir until smooth.

4. When popcorn mixture is cool enough to handle, grease hands with butter or nonstick cooking spray. Shape popcorn mixture into baseball-sized balls; place 1 lollipop stick in each ball. Dip each popcorn ball into melted chocolate and roll in Halloween decorations, if desired. Place on waxed paper until chocolate is set. *Makes 10 to 12 balls*

**Variation:** Pour melted chocolate over caramel popcorn mixture; mix by hand until popcorn is coated with chocolate. Spread evenly on baking sheet lined with waxed paper until chocolate is set.

# Cinnamon-Raisin Roll-Ups

   **4 ounces reduced-fat cream cheese, softened**

   **½ cup shredded carrot**

   **¼ cup golden or regular raisins**

   **1 tablespoon honey**

   **¼ teaspoon ground cinnamon**

   **4 (7- to 8-inch) whole wheat or regular flour tortillas**

   **8 thin apple wedges (optional)**

**1.** Combine cream cheese, carrot, raisins, honey and cinnamon in small bowl; mix well.

**2.** Spread tortillas evenly with cream cheese mixture, leaving ½-inch border around edge of each tortilla. Place 2 apple wedges down center of each tortilla; roll up. Wrap in plastic wrap. Refrigerate until ready to serve or pack in lunch box. *Makes 4 servings*

**Cook's Tip:** For extra convenience, prepare roll-ups the night before. In the morning, pack roll-up in lunch box along with a frozen juice box. The juice box will be thawed by lunchtime and will keep the snack cold in the meantime!

# Indian Corn

¼ cup butter or margarine

1 package (10.5 ounces) mini marshmallows

Yellow food coloring

8 cups peanut butter and chocolate puffed corn cereal

10 lollipop sticks

1 cup candy-coated chocolate pieces

Tan and green raffia

**1.** Line large baking sheet with waxed paper; set aside. Melt butter in large heavy saucepan over low heat. Add marshmallows; stir until melted and smooth. Tint with food coloring until desired shade is reached. Add cereal and ½ cup chocolate pieces; stir until evenly coated. Remove from heat.

**2.** With lightly greased hands, quickly divide mixture into 10 oblong pieces. Push lollipop stick halfway into each oblong piece; shape like ear of corn. Place on prepared baking sheet; press remaining ½ cup chocolate pieces into each "ear." Let treats set.

**3.** Tie or tape raffia to lollipop sticks to resemble corn husks.           *Makes 10 servings*

# Perfect Pita Pizzas

  2 whole wheat or white pita bread rounds
  ½ cup spaghetti or pizza sauce
  ¾ cup (3 ounces) shredded part-skim mozzarella cheese
  1 small zucchini, sliced ¼ inch thick
  ½ small carrot, peeled and sliced
  2 cherry tomatoes, halved
  ¼ small green bell pepper, sliced

**1.** Preheat oven to 375°F. Line baking sheet with foil; set aside.

**2.** Using small scissors, carefully split each pita bread round around edge; separate to form 2 rounds.

**3.** Place rounds, rough sides up, on prepared baking sheet. Bake 5 minutes.

**4.** Spread 2 tablespoons spaghetti sauce onto each round; sprinkle with cheese. Decorate with vegetables to create faces. Bake 10 to 12 minutes or until cheese melts.    *Makes 4 servings*

**Pepperoni Pita Pizzas:** Prepare pita rounds, partially bake, and top with spaghetti sauce and cheese as directed. Place 2 small pepperoni slices on each pizza for eyes. Decorate with cut-up fresh vegetables for rest of face. Continue to bake as directed.

duck    bird    pig

# Inside-Out Turkey Sandwiches

  2 tablespoons fat-free cream cheese

  2 tablespoons pasteurized process cheese spread

  2 teaspoons chopped green onion tops

  1 teaspoon prepared mustard

  12 thin round slices fat-free turkey breast or smoked turkey breast

  4 large pretzel logs or unsalted breadsticks

**1.** Combine cream cheese, process cheese spread, green onion and mustard in small bowl; mix well.

**2.** Arrange 3 turkey slices on large sheet of plastic wrap, overlapping slices in center. Spread ¼ of cream cheese mixture evenly onto turkey slices, covering slices completely. Place 1 pretzel at bottom edge of turkey slices; roll up turkey around pretzel. (Be sure to keep all 3 turkey slices together as you roll them around pretzel.)

**3.** Repeat with remaining ingredients.

*Makes 4 servings*

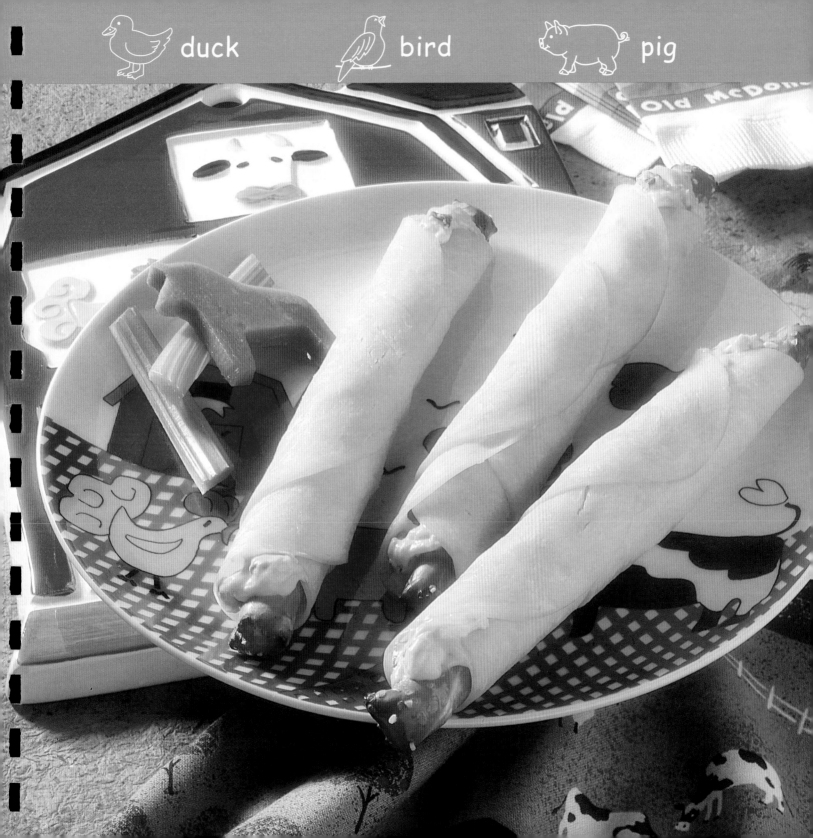

# Quick S'Mores

**1 whole graham cracker**

**1 large marshmallow**

**1 teaspoon hot fudge sauce**

**1.** Break graham cracker in half crosswise. Place one half on small paper plate or microwavable plate; top with marshmallow.

**2.** Spread remaining ½ of cracker with fudge sauce.

**3.** Place cracker with marshmallow in microwave. Microwave at HIGH 12 to 14 seconds or until marshmallow puffs up. Immediately place remaining cracker, fudge side down, over marshmallow. Press crackers gently to even out marshmallow layer. Cool completely.     *Makes 1 serving*

**Cook's Tip:** S'mores can be made the night before and wrapped in plastic wrap or sealed in a small plastic food storage bag. Store at room temperature until ready to pack in your child's lunch box the next morning.

# Coconut Honey Pop Corn Balls

**3 quarts popped JOLLY TIME® Pop Corn**

**¾ cup coconut**

**⅓ cup honey**

**½ teaspoon ground cinnamon**

**Dash of salt**

**3 tablespoons butter or margarine**

Preheat oven to 250°F. Line shallow pan with foil. Place popped pop corn in pan. Keep pop corn warm in oven. Spread coconut in shallow baking pan; toast coconut, stirring once, about 8 to 10 minutes. Combine honey, cinnamon and salt in small saucepan. Heat to boiling; boil 2½ minutes, stirring constantly. Add butter; stir until melted. Pour honey mixture over pop corn. Add coconut. Toss well. Cool just enough to handle. With JOLLY TIME® Pop Corn Ball Maker or buttered hands, shape into balls.     *Makes about 10 pop corn balls*

# Muffin Madness

## Nutty Blueberry Muffins

**1 package DUNCAN HINES® Bakery-Style Wild Maine Blueberry Muffin Mix**
**2 egg whites**
**½ cup water**
**⅓ cup chopped pecans**

**1.** Preheat oven to 400°F. Grease 2½-inch muffin cups (or use paper liners).

**2.** Rinse blueberries from Mix with cold water and drain.

**3.** Pour muffin mix into large bowl. Break up any lumps. Add egg whites and water. Stir until moistened, about 50 strokes. Stir in pecans; fold in blueberries.

**4.** For large muffins, fill cups two-thirds full. Bake at 400°F for 17 to 22 minutes or until toothpick inserted in center comes out clean. (For medium muffins, fill cups half full. Bake at 400°F for 15 to 20 minutes.) Cool in pan 5 to 10 minutes. Loosen carefully before removing from pan. *Makes 8 large or 12 medium muffins*

**Tip:** To reheat leftover muffins, wrap the muffins tightly in foil. Place them in a 400°F oven for 10 to 15 minutes.

158

# Blueberry White Chip Muffins

2 cups all-purpose flour
½ cup granulated sugar
¼ cup packed brown sugar
2½ teaspoons baking powder
½ teaspoon salt
¾ cup milk
1 large egg, lightly beaten
¼ cup butter or margarine, melted
½ teaspoon grated lemon peel
2 cups (12-ounce package) NESTLÉ® TOLL HOUSE® Premier White Morsels, *divided*
1½ cups fresh or frozen blueberries
Streusel Topping (recipe follows)

**PREHEAT** oven to 375°F. Paper-line 18 muffin cups.

**COMBINE** flour, granulated sugar, brown sugar, baking powder and salt in large bowl. Stir in milk, egg, butter and lemon peel. Stir in *1½ cups* morsels and blueberries. Spoon into prepared muffin cups, filling almost full. Sprinkle with Streusel Topping.

**BAKE** for 22 to 25 minutes or until wooden pick inserted in center comes out clean. Cool in pans for 5 minutes; remove to wire racks to cool slightly.

**PLACE** *remaining* morsels in small, *heavy-duty* resealable plastic food storage bag. Microwave on MEDIUM-HIGH (70%) power for 30 seconds; knead. Microwave at additional 10- to 15-second intervals, kneading until smooth. Cut tiny corner from bag; squeeze to drizzle over muffins. Serve warm. *Makes 18 muffins*

**Streusel Topping: COMBINE** ⅓ cup granulated sugar, ¼ cup all-purpose flour and ¼ teaspoon ground cinnamon in small bowl. Cut in 3 tablespoons butter or margarine with pastry blender or two knives until mixture resembles coarse crumbs.

# Peach Gingerbread Muffins

2 cups all-purpose flour

2 teaspoons baking powder

1 teaspoon ground ginger

½ teaspoon salt

½ teaspoon ground cinnamon

¼ teaspoon ground cloves

½ cup sugar

½ cup MOTT'S® Chunky Apple Sauce

¼ cup MOTT'S® Apple Juice

¼ cup GRANDMA'S® Molasses

1 egg

2 tablespoons vegetable oil

1 (16-ounce) can peaches in juice, drained and chopped

1. Preheat oven to 400°F. Line 12 (2½-inch) muffin cups with paper liners or spray with nonstick cooking spray.

2. In large bowl, combine flour, baking powder, ginger, salt and spices.

3. In small bowl, combine sugar, apple sauce, apple juice, molasses, egg and oil.

4. Stir apple sauce mixture into flour mixture just until moistened. Fold in peaches.

5. Spoon batter evenly into prepared muffin cups.

6. Bake 20 minutes or until toothpick inserted in centers comes out clean. Immediately remove from pan; cool on wire rack 10 minutes. Serve warm or cool completely.      *Makes 12 servings*

  F is for frog

# Baked Banana Doughnuts

2 ripe bananas, mashed

2 egg whites

1 tablespoon vegetable oil

1 cup packed brown sugar

1½ cups all-purpose flour

¾ cup whole wheat flour

2 teaspoons baking powder

½ teaspoon baking soda

¼ teaspoon pumpkin pie spice

1 tablespoon granulated sugar

2 tablespoons chopped walnuts (optional)

Preheat oven to 425°F. Spray baking sheet with nonstick cooking spray. Beat bananas, egg whites, oil and brown sugar in large bowl or food processor. Add flours, baking powder, baking soda and pumpkin pie spice. Mix until well blended. Let stand for five minutes for dough to rise. Scoop out heaping tablespoonfuls of dough onto prepared baking sheet. Using thin rubber spatula or butter knife round out doughnut hole in center of dough (if dough sticks to knife or spatula spray with cooking spray). With spatula, smooth outside edges of dough into round doughnut shape. Repeat until all dough is used. Sprinkle with granulated sugar and walnuts, if desired. Bake 6 to 10 minutes or until tops are golden.      *Makes about 22 doughnuts*

**Variation:** Use 8 ounces solid pack pumpkin instead of bananas to make pumpkin doughnuts.

Favorite recipe from **The Sugar Association, Inc.**

## Ice Cream Cone Cupcakes

**1 package (18¼ ounces) white cake mix plus ingredients to prepare**

**2 tablespoons nonpareils***

**2 packages (1¾ ounces each) flat-bottomed ice cream cones (about 24 cones)**

**1 container (16 ounces) vanilla or chocolate frosting**

**Candies and other decorations**

*Nonpareils are tiny, round, brightly colored sprinkles used for cake and cookie decorating.*

**1.** Preheat oven to 350°F.

**2.** Prepare cake mix according to package directions. Stir in nonpareils.

**3.** Spoon ¼ cup batter into each ice cream cone.

**4.** Stand cones on cookie sheet. Bake cones until toothpick inserted into center of cake comes out clean, about 20 minutes. Cool on wire racks.

**5.** Frost each filled cone. Decorate as desired.

*Makes 24 cupcakes*

**Note:** Cupcakes are best served the day they are prepared. Store loosely covered.

## Strawberry Muffins

1¼ cups all-purpose flour

2½ teaspoons baking powder

½ teaspoon salt

1 cup uncooked old-fashioned oats

½ cup sugar

1 cup milk

½ cup butter, melted

1 egg, beaten

1 teaspoon vanilla

1 cup chopped fresh strawberries

Preheat oven to 425°F. Grease 12 (2½-inch) muffin cups; set aside.

Combine flour, baking powder and salt in large bowl. Stir in oats and sugar. Combine milk, butter, egg and vanilla in small bowl until well blended; stir into flour mixture just until moistened. Fold in strawberries. Spoon into prepared muffin cups, filling about two-thirds full.

Bake 15 to 18 minutes or until lightly browned and toothpick inserted in center comes out clean. Remove from pan. Cool on wire rack 10 minutes. Serve warm or cool completely.

*Makes 12 muffins*

# Mocha-Macadamia Nut Muffins

1¼ cups all-purpose flour

⅔ cup sugar

2½ tablespoons unsweetened cocoa powder

1 teaspoon baking soda

¼ teaspoon salt

⅔ cup buttermilk*

3 tablespoons margarine or butter, melted

1 egg, beaten

1 tablespoon instant coffee granules, dissolved in 1 tablespoon hot water

¾ teaspoon vanilla

½ cup coarsely chopped macadamia nuts

Powdered sugar (optional)

*You can substitute soured fresh milk. To sour milk, place 2 teaspoons lemon juice plus enough milk to equal ⅔ cup in 2-cup measure. Stir; let stand 5 minutes before using.

Preheat oven to 400°F. Grease or paper-line 12 (2½-inch) muffin cups.

Combine flour, sugar, cocoa powder, baking soda and salt in large bowl. Whisk together buttermilk, margarine, egg, coffee mixture and vanilla in small bowl until blended. Stir into flour mixture just until moistened. Fold in macadamia nuts. Spoon evenly into prepared muffin cups.

Bake 13 to 17 minutes or until toothpick inserted into centers comes out clean. Cool in muffin pan on wire rack 5 minutes. Remove from pan and cool on wire rack 10 minutes. Sprinkle with powdered sugar, if desired. *Makes 12 muffins*

# Old-Fashioned Cake Doughnuts

3¾ cups all-purpose flour

1 tablespoon baking powder

1 teaspoon ground cinnamon

¾ teaspoon salt

½ teaspoon ground nutmeg

3 eggs

¾ cup granulated sugar

1 cup applesauce

2 tablespoons butter, melted

1 quart vegetable oil

2 cups sifted powdered sugar

3 tablespoons milk

½ teaspoon vanilla

Colored sprinkles (optional)

Combine flour, baking powder, cinnamon, salt and nutmeg in medium bowl. Beat eggs in large bowl with electric mixer at high speed until frothy. Gradually beat in granulated sugar. Continue beating at high speed 4 minutes until thick and lemon colored, scraping down side of bowl once. Reduce speed to low; beat in applesauce and butter.

Beat in flour mixture until well blended. Divide dough into halves. Place each half on large piece of plastic wrap. Pat each half into 5-inch square; wrap in plastic wrap. Refrigerate 3 hours or until well chilled.

To prepare glaze, stir together powdered sugar, milk and vanilla in small bowl until smooth. Cover; set aside.

Roll out 1 dough half to ⅜-inch thickness. Cut dough with floured 3-inch doughnut cutter; repeat with remaining dough. Reserve doughnut holes. Reroll scraps; cut dough again. Pour oil into large Dutch oven. Place deep-fry thermometer in oil. Heat oil over medium heat until thermometer registers 375°F. Adjust heat as necessary to maintain temperature at 375°F.

Place 4 doughnuts and holes in hot oil. Cook 2 minutes or until golden brown, turning often. Remove with slotted spoon; drain on paper towels. Repeat with remaining doughnuts and holes. Spread glaze over warm doughnuts; decorate with sprinkles, if desired.

*Makes 12 doughnuts and holes*

# Gingerbread Streusel Raisin Muffins

    1 cup raisins

    ½ cup boiling water

    ⅓ cup margarine or butter, softened

    ¾ cup GRANDMA'S® Molasses (Unsulphured)

    1 egg

    2 cups all-purpose flour

 1½ teaspoons baking soda

    1 teaspoon cinnamon

    1 teaspoon ginger

    ½ teaspoon salt

**Topping**

    ⅓ cup all-purpose flour

    ¼ cup firmly packed brown sugar

    ¼ cup chopped nuts

    3 tablespoons margarine or butter

    1 teaspoon cinnamon

Preheat oven to 375°F. Grease bottoms only of 12 muffin cups or line with paper baking cups. In small bowl, cover raisins with boiling water; let stand 5 minutes. In large bowl, beat ⅓ cup margarine and molasses until fluffy. Add egg; beat well. Stir in 2 cups flour, baking soda, 1 teaspoon cinnamon, ginger and salt. Blend just until dry ingredients are moistened. Gently stir in raisins and water. Fill prepared muffin cups ¾ full. For topping, combine all ingredients in small bowl. Sprinkle over muffins.

Bake 20 to 25 minutes or until toothpick inserted in centers comes out clean. Cool 5 minutes; remove from pan. Serve warm. *Makes 12 muffins*

Gingerbread Streusel
Raisin Muffins

# Blueberry Cheesecake Muffins

8 ounces cream cheese, softened

1 cup plus 1 tablespoon no-calorie sugar substitute for baking, divided

2 eggs

1 teaspoon grated lemon peel

1 teaspoon vanilla

¾ cup bran flakes cereal

½ cup all-purpose flour

½ cup soy flour

2 teaspoons baking powder

¼ teaspoon salt

¾ cup milk

3 tablespoons melted butter

4 tablespoons no-sugar-added blueberry fruit spread

½ teaspoon ground cinnamon

1. Preheat oven to 350°F. Spray 12 muffin cups with nonstick cooking spray.

2. Beat cream cheese in medium bowl at high speed of electric mixer until smooth. Beat in ¾ cup sugar substitute, 1 egg, lemon peel and vanilla.

3. Stir together cereal, flours, ¼ cup sugar substitute, baking powder and salt in medium bowl. In separate small bowl, whisk milk, butter and 1 egg until blended; pour over cereal mixture. Mix gently just until blended.

4. Spoon about 2 tablespoons batter into each muffin cup. Spread 1 teaspoon fruit spread over batter. Spread cream cheese mixture over fruit spread. Combine remaining 1 tablespoon sugar substitute and cinnamon; sprinkle mixture evenly over cream cheese mixture.

5. Bake 30 to 35 minutes or until toothpick inserted into centers comes out clean. Cool muffins 10 minutes in pan on wire rack. Remove muffins from pan and cool. Serve warm or at room temperature. Refrigerate leftover muffins. *Makes 12 muffins*

# Apple Butter Spice Muffins

½ **cup sugar**

1 **teaspoon ground cinnamon**

¼ **teaspoon ground nutmeg**

⅛ **teaspoon ground allspice**

½ **cup pecans or walnuts, chopped**

2 **cups all-purpose flour**

2 **teaspoons baking powder**

¼ **teaspoon salt**

1 **cup milk**

¼ **cup vegetable oil**

1 **egg**

¼ **cup apple butter**

1. Preheat oven to 400°F. Grease or paper-line 12 (2½-inch) muffin cups.

2. Combine sugar, cinnamon, nutmeg and allspice in large bowl. Toss 2 tablespoons sugar mixture with pecans in small bowl; set aside. Add flour, baking powder and salt to remaining sugar mixture.

3. Combine milk, oil and egg in medium bowl. Stir into flour mixture just until moistened.

4. Spoon 1 tablespoon batter into each prepared muffin cup. Spoon 1 teaspoon apple butter into each cup. Spoon remaining batter evenly over apple butter. Sprinkle reserved pecan mixture over each muffin. Bake 20 to 25 minutes or until golden brown and toothpick inserted in center comes out clean. Immediately remove from pan; cool on wire rack 10 minutes. Serve warm or cold.

*Makes 12 muffins*

**Apple Butter Spice Muffins**

# White Chocolate Chunk Muffins

2½ cups all-purpose flour

1 cup packed brown sugar

⅓ cup unsweetened cocoa powder

2 teaspoons baking soda

½ teaspoon salt

1⅓ cups buttermilk

6 tablespoons butter, melted

2 eggs, beaten

1½ teaspoons vanilla

1½ cups chopped white chocolate

Preheat oven to 400°F. Grease 12 (3½-inch) large muffin cups; set aside.

Combine flour, sugar, cocoa, baking soda and salt in large bowl. Combine buttermilk, butter, eggs and vanilla in small bowl until blended. Stir into flour mixture just until moistened. Fold in white chocolate. Spoon into prepared muffin cups, filling half full.

Bake 25 to 30 minutes or until toothpick inserted into centers comes out clean. Cool in pan on wire rack 5 minutes. Remove from pan. Cool on wire rack 10 minutes. Serve warm or cool completely.

*Makes 12 jumbo muffins*

# Chunky Apple Molasses Muffins

**2 cups all-purpose flour**

**¼ cup sugar**

**1 tablespoon baking powder**

**1 teaspoon ground cinnamon**

**¼ teaspoon salt**

**1 Fuji apple, peeled, cored and finely chopped**

**½ cup milk**

**¼ cup vegetable oil**

**¼ cup molasses**

**1 large egg**

**1.** Heat oven to 450°F. Lightly grease eight 3-inch muffin pan cups. In large bowl, combine flour, sugar, baking powder, cinnamon and salt. Add apple and stir to distribute evenly.

**2.** In small bowl, beat together milk, oil, molasses and egg. Stir into dry ingredients and mix just until blended. Fill muffin pan cups with batter. Bake 5 minutes. Reduce heat to 350°F; bake 12 to 15 minutes longer or until centers of muffins spring back when gently pressed. Cool in pan 5 minutes. Remove muffins from pan and cool slightly; serve warm.     *Makes 8 (3-inch) muffins*

Favorite recipe from **Washington Apple Commission**

## Gingerbread Pear Muffins

1¾ cups all-purpose flour

⅓ cup sugar

2 teaspoons baking powder

¾ teaspoon ground ginger

¼ teaspoon baking soda

¼ teaspoon salt

¼ teaspoon ground cinnamon

⅓ cup milk

¼ cup vegetable oil

¼ cup light molasses

1 egg

1 medium pear, peeled, cored and finely chopped

**1.** Preheat oven to 375°F. Grease or paper-line 12 (2½-inch) muffin cups.

**2.** Sift flour, sugar, baking powder, ginger, baking soda, salt and cinnamon into large bowl.

**3.** Combine milk, oil, molasses and egg in medium bowl. Stir in pear. Stir milk mixture into flour mixture just until moistened.

**4.** Spoon evenly into prepared muffin cups, filling ⅔ full.

**5.** Bake 20 minutes or until toothpick inserted into centers comes out clean. Immediately remove from pan; cool on wire rack 10 minutes. Serve warm or cold. *Makes 12 muffins*

# Blueberry Muffins

 1 cup fresh or thawed, frozen blueberries
 1¾ cups plus 1 tablespoon all-purpose flour, divided
 2 teaspoons baking powder
 1 teaspoon grated lemon peel
 ½ teaspoon salt
 ½ cup MOTT'S® Apple Sauce
 ½ cup sugar
 1 whole egg
 1 egg white
 2 tablespoons vegetable oil
 ¼ cup skim milk

**1.** Preheat oven to 375°F. Line 12 (2½-inch) muffin cups with paper liners or spray with nonstick cooking spray.

**2.** In small bowl, toss blueberries with 1 tablespoon flour.

**3.** In large bowl, combine remaining 1¾ cups flour, baking powder, lemon peel and salt.

**4.** In another small bowl, combine apple sauce, sugar, whole egg, egg white and oil.

**5.** Stir apple sauce mixture into flour mixture alternately with milk. Mix just until moistened. Fold in blueberry mixture.

**6.** Spoon evenly into prepared muffin cups.

**7.** Bake 20 minutes or until toothpick inserted in centers comes out clean. Immediately remove from pan; cool on wire rack 10 minutes. Serve warm or cool completely.          *Makes 12 servings*

# Acknowledgments

## The publisher would like to thank the companies and organizations listed below for the use of their recipes and photographs in this publication.

California Dried Plum Board

Duncan Hines® and Moist Deluxe®
are registered trademarks of Aurora Foods Inc.

Eagle Brand®

Grandma's® is a registered trademark of Mott's, Inc.

Hershey Foods Corporation

JOLLY TIME® Pop Corn

© Mars, Incorporated 2004

Mott's® is a registered trademark of Mott's, Inc.

Nestlé USA

The J.M. Smucker Company

The Sugar Association, Inc.

Texas Peanut Producers Board

Walnut Marketing Board

Washington Apple Commission

# Index

# METRIC CONVERSION CHART

## VOLUME MEASUREMENTS (dry)

1/8 teaspoon = 0.5 mL
1/4 teaspoon = 1 mL
1/2 teaspoon = 2 mL
3/4 teaspoon = 4 mL
1 teaspoon = 5 mL
1 tablespoon = 15 mL
2 tablespoons = 30 mL
1/4 cup = 60 mL
1/3 cup = 75 mL
1/2 cup = 125 mL
2/3 cup = 150 mL
3/4 cup = 175 mL
1 cup = 250 mL
2 cups = 1 pint = 500 mL
3 cups = 750 mL
4 cups = 1 quart = 1 L

## VOLUME MEASUREMENTS (fluid)

1 fluid ounce (2 tablespoons) = 30 mL
4 fluid ounces (1/2 cup) = 125 mL
8 fluid ounces (1 cup) = 250 mL
12 fluid ounces (1 1/2 cups) = 375 mL
16 fluid ounces (2 cups) = 500 mL

## WEIGHTS (mass)

1/2 ounce = 15 g
1 ounce = 30 g
3 ounces = 90 g
4 ounces = 120 g
8 ounces = 225 g
10 ounces = 285 g
12 ounces = 360 g
16 ounces = 1 pound = 450 g

## DIMENSIONS

1/16 inch = 2 mm
1/8 inch = 3 mm
1/4 inch = 6 mm
1/2 inch = 1.5 cm
3/4 inch = 2 cm
1 inch = 2.5 cm

## OVEN TEMPERATURES

250°F = 120°C
275°F = 140°C
300°F = 150°C
325°F = 160°C
350°F = 180°C
375°F = 190°C
400°F = 200°C
425°F = 220°C
450°F = 230°C

## BAKING PAN SIZES

| Utensil | Size in Inches/Quarts | Metric Volume | Size in Centimeters |
|---|---|---|---|
| Baking or Cake Pan (square or rectangular) | 8×8×2 | 2 L | 20×20×5 |
| | 9×9×2 | 2.5 L | 23×23×5 |
| | 12×8×2 | 3 L | 30×20×5 |
| | 13×9×2 | 3.5 L | 33×23×5 |
| Loaf Pan | 8×4×3 | 1.5 L | 20×10×7 |
| | 9×5×3 | 2 L | 23×13×7 |
| Round Layer Cake Pan | 8×1½ | 1.2 L | 20×4 |
| | 9×1½ | 1.5 L | 23×4 |
| Pie Plate | 8×1¼ | 750 mL | 20×3 |
| | 9×1¼ | 1 L | 23×3 |
| Baking Dish or Casserole | 1 quart | 1 L | — |
| | 1½ quart | 1.5 L | — |
| | 2 quart | 2 L | — |